T0311779

"A much-needed scholarly contribution to understanding how Dominican American communities, defying exclusion, and daringly engaging local, state, and federal structures of civic participation, have developed a collective political muscle in the Northeastern United States during the last half-century, changing the ethnic political landscape of a megacity like New York. Blending institutional analysis and ethnography, Jiménez Polanco's work sets a path for future studies that should further deepen her findings. A very welcome tool for those trying to teach Dominican Studies in U.S. higher education today."

Anthony Stevens-Acevedo, Historian, former Assistant Director of the CUNY Dominican Studies Institute

"In *Dominican American Politics: Immigrants, Activists, and Politicians* Jacqueline Jiménez Polanco presents the most complete narrative to date about Dominicans' involvement in U.S. politics. This is a mature writing by an author who has experienced, observed, and patiently studied the process of politization undertaken by the Dominican people in the United States. Jiménez Polanco's discussion brings attention to the relationship between the development of leadership and rooted, established communities on U.S. soil, and how both became stakeholders with whom the other ethnic and interest groups need to negotiate and reckon with. Taking into account Juan Rodríguez, Jiménez Polanco portrays the Dominican political leadership in the U.S. as decisive and assertive, conscientious and meticulous in demarcating and marking the spaces where it gravitates. This book goes through the politization of Dominicans with ease, from spontaneous community activism to formal organizing and recording, and the rise of electoral politics in Dominican-dominated spaces and beyond. In a challenging conclusion that seeks to materialize a tacit assumption, Jiménez Polanco argues convincingly that the ancestral land's steady and strong tradition of political involvement influenced the birth of Dominican political participation in the U.S."

Ramona Hernández, Professor of Sociology and Director of the CUNY Dominican Studies Institute

Dominican American Politics

In this book, Jacqueline Jiménez Polanco examines the politics of empowerment of Dominican Americans in the United States. Covering the first two decades of the twenty-first century, Jiménez Polanco provides a new analytical perspective to understand the political development of a growing ethnic community that has been historically neglected in the studies of Latino/a/x political development and whose peculiar characteristics represent a paradigmatic case that debunks pervading theories about immigrant communities' participation and representation in U.S. electoral politics. Rich archival research and interviews with key Dominican American leaders and activists shed light on how some patterns followed by Dominican Americans in their political empowerment correspond to those of other Latino/a/x communities, while other patterns distinctly diverge from that common trend. *Dominican American Politics: Immigrants, Activists, and Politicians* serves as a perfect companion for courses on Latino/a/x and Dominican studies and U.S. ethnic politics.

Jacqueline Jiménez Polanco is Associate Professor of Sociology at Bronx Community College of the City University of New York (CUNY). She holds a Ph.D. in political science and sociology from the Universidad Complutense de Madrid with a concentration in political changes in contemporary democracies. Dr. Jiménez Polanco is the author of *Los partidos políticos en la República Dominicana: Actividad electoral y desarrollo organizativo* and *Corrupción y cartelización de la política en la República Dominicana* and co-editor of *Dominican Politics in the Twenty First Century: Continuity and Change*. She was granted a PSC-CUNY Award in 2023.

Routledge Research in American Politics and Governance

For more information about this series, please visit: www.routledge.com/Routledge-
Research-in-American-Politics-and-Governance/book-series/RRAPG

Dominican American Politics

Immigrants, Activists, and
Politicians

Jacqueline Jiménez Polanco

Routledge
Taylor & Francis Group

NEW YORK AND LONDON

First published 2024
by Routledge
605 Third Avenue, New York, NY 10158

and by Routledge
4 Park Square, Milton Park, Abingdon, Oxon, OX14 4RN

Routledge is an imprint of the Taylor & Francis Group, an informa business

Library of Congress Cataloging-in-Publication Data
Names: Jiménez Polanco, Jacqueline, author.
Title: Dominican American politics : immigrants, activists, and politicians / Jacqueline Jiménez Polanco.
Description: New York, NY : Routledge, 2024. |
Series: Routledge research in American politics and governance |
Includes bibliographical references and index. |
Summary: "In this book, Jacqueline Jiménez Polanco examines the politics of empowerment of Dominican Americans in the United States. Covering the first two decades of the twenty-first century, Jiménez Polanco provides a new analytical perspective to understand the political development of a growing ethnic community that has been historically neglected in the studies of Latinx political development and whose peculiar characteristics represent a paradigmatic case that debunks pervading theories about immigrant communities' participation and representation in U.S. electoral politics. Rich archival research and interviews with key Dominican American leaders and activists shed light on how some patterns followed by Dominican Americans in their political empowerment correspond to those of other Latinx communities, while other patterns distinctly diverge from that common trend. Dominican American Politics: Immigrants, Activists, and Politicians serves as a perfect companion for courses on Latinx and Dominican studies, and U.S. ethnic politics"– Provided by publisher.
Identifiers: LCCN 2024005912 (print) | LCCN 2024005913 (ebook) |
ISBN 9781032770307 (hardback) | ISBN 9781003497455 (ebook)
Subjects: LCSH: Dominican Americans–Politics and government. |
Dominican Americans–Political activity–History–21st century.
Classification: LCC E184.D6 J564 2024 (print) | LCC E184.D6 (ebook) |
DDC 320.089687293073–dc23/eng/20240313
LC record available at https://lccn.loc.gov/2024005912
LC ebook record available at https://lccn.loc.gov/2024005913

ISBN: 978-1-032-77030-7 (hbk)
ISBN: 978-1-032-81475-9 (pbk)
ISBN: 978-1-003-49745-5 (ebk)

DOI: 10.4324/9781003497455

Typeset in Times New Roman
by Newgen Publishing UK

In loving memory of my mother, Juana María Polanco, who instilled in me the love for teaching and writing at an early age.

To my students, whose inquisitive discussions about the Dominican American people have inspired me to write this book.

Contents

Figures

Tables

Acknowledgments

I am deeply grateful to my friend and colleague Dr. Ernesto Sagás who, as my copyeditor, provided propitious ideas and revised my work with a candid enthusiasm that allowed me to complete this manuscript before the planned submission date.

I would also like to thank the CUNY Dominican Studies Institute (DSI) for awarding me a fellowship to conduct research for this book. My sincere gratitude goes to Director Dr. Ramona Hernández and DSI staff members Sarah Aponte, Jhensen Ortiz, and Jessy Pérez for guiding me through the treasured resources of the CUNY DSI Library and Archives. I would also like to acknowledge the funding provided by a PSC-CUNY Award, jointly founded by the Professional Staff Congress and the City University of New York. I am also thankful to my colleagues at the Social Sciences Department of Bronx Community College for their precious support to my application for a sabbatical leave that gave me the time, serenity, and mobility to conduct research, carry out interviews, and write the manuscript in the pleasant settings of New York City and Santiago (Dominican Republic). Many thanks to my friend, historian Anthony Stevens-Acevedo, and all the elected and appointed officials, political advisors, and activists who generously participated in interviews for this book: U.S. Congressman Adriano Espaillat, Commissioner Guillermo Linares, Commissioner Ydanis Rodríguez, Councilwoman Carmen De La Rosa, Councilman Oswald Feliz, State Senator Ana Quezada, Raysa Castillo, Lilliam Pérez, and Raquel Batista.

The completion of this book would not have been possible without the enthusiasm and support of my relatives in the United States and the Dominican Republic: Venecia, Daniel, Nova, Rudy, Jaslynn, Juliet, Marleny, Rodolfo, Maritza, and Onofre.

Prologue

Dominican Americans Have Finally Arrived

Ernesto Sagás

Something significant happened to Dominicans in the United States around the turn of the century: they became Americans. Of course, Dominican immigrants have been becoming Americans since there have been Dominicans in the United States of America. What I really mean to say is that a community that for long had been imagined as recently arrived and mostly made up of immigrants with tenuous connections to U.S. society, was finally being perceived as becoming integrated into the U.S. political system by the late twentieth century/early twenty-first century. In that sense, for the U.S. political mainstream, Dominicans had become Americans—or more specifically, Dominican Americans. Even the academic literature reflected this trend. Whereas from the 1970s to 1990s, most academic works examined different aspects of the Dominican migratory experience to the United States (Aponte 1999), by the turn of the century, academic monographs about the Dominican American community began to emerge (Torres-Saillant and Hernández 1998). It is in this context that the current work takes place. Jacqueline Jiménez Polanco's study about the political empowerment of Dominican Americans is the right heir to a proud tradition of works on a community that was little known outside of New York City and its environs. Until now.

As the Dominican community increased in size to become the fourth largest Latino/a/x community (after Mexicans, Puerto Ricans, and Cubans) by the millennium, scholars—and politicians—began taking notice. And as the first immigrant generation began naturalizing as U.S. citizens and a second generation of children born in the United States came of age, Dominican Americans started making headways into New York City politics, then New York state politics, and finally, regional and national politics with the election of Dominican Americans to elective positions in other states of the

Northeast, and finally, the election of Adriano Espaillat to the U.S. House of Representatives in 2016. With one of their own (and a naturalized immigrant to boot) serving in the corridors of power in Washington, D.C., Dominicans now can say that mainstream America knows who they are. They have finally arrived.

But few people outside of the Dominican American community really know *how* they arrived. How did Dominicans move from a community of immigrants to a community of Americans? From the politics of the homeland to U.S. politics? From political outsiders to political insiders? In *Dominican American Politics: Immigrants, Activists, and Politicians,* Jacqueline Jiménez Polanco provides us with the first comprehensive study of the political evolution of Dominicans in the United States, as they joined the ranks of other immigrant communities and became an integral part of the American polity. Like other transnational immigrant cohorts in the United States (Sagás and Molina 2004), Dominicans are a multilayered community, with several waves of political exiles and immigrants arriving at different stages throughout the twentieth century (but particularly after the 1960s) and including generations of U.S.-born children and naturalized U.S. citizens. Hailing from a Latin American nation where political mobilization and participation were on the rise, it came as no surprise that Dominicans sought to express themselves politically to the extent that the political setting in the host country allowed them, from the participation of undocumented Dominican immigrants in New York City's Area Policy Boards and Community School Boards to the present-day mobilization of a Dominican American voting bloc in New York's 13th congressional district. The complex legal, socioeconomic, and political picture of a transnational community in transition is deftly detailed in this scholarly examination of Dominican American politics by Jiménez Polanco, from the first, tentative steps of a community seeking entry into the system to the assertive ethnic politics of a well-established constituency.

Moreover, Jiménez Polanco's book includes interviews with veteran and younger Dominican American political leaders—a valuable primary source that provides the reader with insights into the mindset, strategies, and goals of two generations of Dominican Americans making their first forays into U.S. politics. Their triumphs and failures, the lessons learned, and the political evolution of the Dominican American community are well documented through the voices of those who were there. Some of them, with two to three decades of public service and political experience under their sleeves, reflect in hindsight on those key moments that turned political corners for Dominican Americans, whereas the younger ones emphasize the importance of working with diverse ethnic coalitions in order to expand the political reach of the Dominican American community beyond the confines of Northern Manhattan and the Bronx.

Finally, *Dominican American Politics: Immigrants, Activists, and Politicians* is a key resource for those engaged in the comparative study of Latino/a/x and U.S. ethnic politics. Jiménez Polanco analyzes what made Dominicans so unique vis-à-vis other Latino/a/x/ethnic groups in New York City politics, while at the same time portraying the traditional hurdles that most communities of color face as part of their journey toward political empowerment. In that sense, she shows how Dominicans traveled down a familiar political path but did so in their own way. The book is sure to become a must-read introduction to the Dominican American community in general and its politics in particular and a foundational text for future studies of this emerging ethnic constituency. For if there is one thing that we can be sure about, is that Dominican Americans are just getting started. Their political ascent in New York, Northeast, and U.S. politics will continue unabated as their numbers, presence, and political involvement grow in the region.

Introduction

Dominican Migration to the United States and Political Activism

In the uppermost part of Manhattan, from 159th Street in Washington Heights to 218th Street in Inwood, there is a three-mile stretch of Broadway that was officially named Juan Rodríguez on May 16, 2013. The name honors a free mulatto man from Santo Domingo, born in the eastern side of the island of Hispaniola (present-day Dominican Republic), who became the first non-native immigrant to ever settle in the island of Manhattan in 1613. Rodríguez came to Manhattan aboard a Dutch vessel and learned the Algonquian language of the Lenape people, became a prosperous entrepreneur, and married a woman from the community (Stevens-Acevedo, Weterings, and Álvarez Francés 2013). Inspired by the story surrounding the unearthing of Rodríguez's arrival and his permanent settlement in today's New York City by historian Anthony Stevens-Acevedo from the CUNY Dominican Studies Institute, the young actor Armando Batista co-wrote and performed the play entitled "I am New York: Juan Rodríguez."[1] According to research led by Ramona Hernández from the CUNY Dominican Institute, from 1892 to 1924, an estimated 5,000 Dominicans came to New York City through Ellis Island (Santana and Aponte 2019), and many of them settled in Washington Heights and Harlem with the idea of staying permanently.[2] From 1916 to the 1950s Dominicans migrated to the United States as political exiles during the first U.S. military occupation of the country and the dictatorial Trujillo regime. Over 300 years after Juan Rodríguez's immigrant journey, Dominicans came in mass to New York City in the early 1960s, and most of them settled, as Juan Rodríguez did, in Manhattan. But starting in the 1990s, Dominican Americans began relocating to several other cities throughout the United States.

DOI: 10.4324/9781003497455-1

In this book, readers will come to realize that most Dominican American leaders and their constituents are as much a part of New York as Juan Rodríguez was but also that due to the increase in the cost of living, gentrification, and forced displacements, many Dominicans have progressively relocated to other U.S. states, particularly along the East coast, including Rhode Island, New Jersey, Massachusetts, Maryland, Connecticut, Pennsylvania, and Florida, where they have established socioeconomic and political enclaves that have allowed them to elect local and state officials. The first massive wave of Dominican migrants to the United States that took place in the early 1960s followed a convulsive era after the assassination of ruthless dictator Rafael Trujillo in 1961, the breakdown of the country's first democratic transition as the result of a military coup against Pres. Juan Bosch in 1963, the 1965 civil war caused by the attempt at reinstating Bosch's democratic government and the second U.S. military occupation that smothered the civil war that same year, and U.S. support for the election of authoritarian Pres. Joaquín Balaguer (Trujillo's former puppet) in 1966. The U.S. government saw Bosch's leftist policies as a threat to its Cold War anti-communist geopolitical stance, and during Bosch's ephemeral presidency, the U.S. Consulate in Santo Domingo granted a large number of tourist visas that allowed many Dominicans to travel to the United States, a policy that continued after its military occupation of the Dominican Republic. These events took place as the U.S. Immigration and Nationality Act of 1965 allowed entry to immigrants other than Northwestern Europeans, significantly altering immigration demographics in the United States for the first time since its foundation in 1776. The signing of this act by Pres. Lyndon B. Johnson was followed by an open-door policy that allowed immigration into the United States for many non-Whites during a time in which 84% of the U.S. population consisted of non-Hispanic Whites.

The tourist-visa status of most Dominicans who entered the United States in the early 1960s prompted the establishment of a community composed mainly of undocumented immigrants with little access to education and limited socioeconomic resources, significant hurdles to the achievement of economic progress and the American dream, as well as to participation in local and national politics. Therefore, it was several decades before Dominican immigrants organized themselves and participated collectively in U.S. institutions through New York City's Area Policy Boards (APBs) and Community School Boards (CSBs) (particularly in District 6 of Manhattan), for which U.S. permanent residence or citizenship was not required. The APBs and CSBs became an incubator for development of future political leaders, and the persistent community activism of Dominicans facilitated the election of María Luna as the first Dominican female district leader in the 1970s and Julio Hernández as the first Dominican male district leader in the early 1980s. In the early 1990s, Guillermo Linares, who was a public schoolteacher, became the first Dominican to be elected to the New York City Council, Key Palacios was the first Dominican American councilwoman elected in New Jersey, and Adriano Espaillat became the first Dominican-born New York State assemblymember. The political experience acquired in the CSBs allowed Dominican leaders to participate in the City's political redistricting process and eventually make it to the lower levels of the Democratic Party's state committees. Dominicans progressively developed solid links with the Democratic party machinery and increased their political representation to forty-eight elected officials from 2013 to 2023, including the election of Adriano Espaillat as the first Dominican-born representative to the United States Congress in 2016.

Mainly located in the East coast of the United States, Dominican American politicians and community activists have been actively engaged in the naturalization and voting registration of their constituents, thus guaranteeing their access to elective positions within the Democratic Party via the progressive increase of Dominican voters. In essence, the Dominican community in the United States produces leaders and mobilizes voters, which become the catalyst for U.S. major party organizations to recruit them as potentially successful candidates and active voters. In addition, Dominican American leaders have historically developed strong links with other ethnic minorities, such as African Americans and Puerto Ricans, and White communities such as Jewish Americans and Irish Americans, that share with them an advocacy for issues concerning quality education, good-paying jobs, affordable housing, accessible health care, and progressive immigration policies (among other major demands).[3]

This book analyzes the development and consolidation of Dominican American political empowerment throughout five chapters. Chapter 1 examines the international political activity of Dominican exiles in the United States during the first three quarters of the twentieth century in response to the first U.S. occupation of the country and Rafael Trujillo's and Joaquín Balaguer's authoritarian regimes. It also includes a detailed analysis of the early incorporation of Dominicans into U.S. politics in the early 1980s and 1990s via their community activism in the APBs and CSBs. Chapter 2 discusses the role of community organizations in the engagement of Dominicans in the U.S. electoral process, with particular attention to the work of the Dominican American National Roundtable (DANRT), Dominicanos USA (DUSA), and Dominicans 2000. It also highlights the development of the long-standing political leadership of Ydanis Rodríguez and Adriano Espaillat, as well as the emergence of new leaders and their confrontations with old leaders, epitomized by the conflict between Marisol Alcántara and Adriano Espaillat. In addition, this chapter reviews U.S. census data and the demographic and socioeconomic characteristics of the Dominican American population and their effect on electoral processes. Chapter 3 focuses on contrasting the Dominican American political experience with that of other Latino/a/x communities (including Puerto Ricans, Mexicans, and Cubans) and examines how some elements of their political empowerment influence Dominican Americans and how the Dominican experience could serve as a role model for other Latino/a/x communities. Chapter 4 delves into the challenges and accomplishments of Dominican American elected officials from New York and Rhode Island, based on interviews with Adriano Espaillat, Guillermo Linares, Ydanis Rodríguez, Carmen De La Rosa, and Ana Quezada. Chapter 5 presents an overview of the main aspects of current Dominican American political involvement, including their fast-growing representation and activism in Rhode Island that allowed them to present two female candidates running for Congress: Sabina Matos and Ana Quezada. It also examines the prospects of Dominican Americans in U.S. politics, including racial/ethnic politics, the relationship between leaders and constituents, and the main contributions of Dominican Americans to American society and its political system.

The book was made possible thanks to access to archival materials at the CUNY Dominican Studies Institute, interviews with Dominican American political leaders, advisors, and community activists; and the current literature on Dominicans and other Latinos/as/xs in U.S. politics. The book also represents a well-timed contribution to the study of Latino/a/x politics in the United States. On the one hand, it fills a gap in the Latino/a/x studies literature, in which most of the academic studies concentrate on the analysis of Mexicans, Puerto Ricans, and Cubans, to the exclusion of Dominicans, as observed in Chapter 3 (Huddy, Mason, and Horwitz 2016, Leighley and Nagler 2016, Sears,

Danbold, and Zavala 2016, and Potochnick and Stegmaier 2020, among others). On the other hand, the emphasis of this book on Dominican American electoral politics in the United States is long overdue as academic books published during the first decade of this century do not cover this topic. Instead, their analysis focuses on Dominican activism in the 1990s as exemplified in small businesses (Ricourt 2002), community networks in the 1990s (Aparicio 2006), and business owners and political and cultural associations (Krohn-Hansen 2012). In addition, as highlighted in this book, the last decade constitutes a turning point in Dominican American political representation, as it has produced a considerable increase in the number of elected officials, that more than doubled its size since the early 2000s, which in turn reflects the growing electoral participation of the Dominican American community, debunking the engrained stereotype that Dominicans did not want to become U.S. citizens and did not care about American politics. Indeed, this development attests to the fact that Dominicans come from a highly politically involved homeland and that as soon as they found a chance to engage in political activism in the United States, they never let go of it. Moreover, Dominicans also made sure that they would be able to keep their political rights back home, so they supported dual citizenship, which has allowed Dominicans to build a strong connection with American society while greatly contributing to the socioeconomic improvement of the Dominican Republic, thus shaping a bilateral-transnational experience that could serve as a role model for other immigrant communities in the United States and elsewhere. My goals with this book are: first, to bring U.S. academia closer to the Dominican American community; and second, that U.S. scholars and college students could find in this book concise ideas to better understand the development of Dominican American political engagement in the United States.

Notes

1 See, www.nbcnews.com/news/latino/new-yorks-first-immigrant-meet-juan-rodriguez-n114771 www.nypl.org/audiovideo/teenlive-presents-i-am-new-york-juan-rodriguez-bronx-library-center
2 Presentation by Dr. Ramona Hernández at the Dominican Cultural Club, Bronx Community College, May 27, 2014. See https://en.wikipedia.org/wiki/Dominican_Americans
3 While writing this introduction on November 21, 2023, breaking news caused anguish among those who defend the voting rights of racial and

ethnic minorities. The 8th Circuit Court of Appeals (based in St. Louis and controlled by Republicans) ruled that private individuals and groups such as the NAACP (i.e., the National Association for the Advancement of Colored People) do not have the ability to sue under Section 2 of the federal Voting Rights Act. Only the U.S. Attorney General can enforce that key section, which requires political maps to include districts where the preferred candidates of minority populations can win elections. This decision contradicts decades of precedent and could further erode protections under the landmark 1965 civil rights law that was born from the violent struggle for the right of African Americans to freely cast ballots. It dismissed a case brought by the NAACP Arkansas State Conference and the Arkansas Public Policy Panel in which they were rejecting a state's redistricting plan that created eleven majority-Black districts, instead of sixteen, which according to the NAACP more closely mirror the state's demographics. Should this decision stand, it would mark a setback of the enforcement of the electoral law that led to increased minority power and representation in American politics. See "Federal appeals court deals a blow to Voting Rights Act, ruling that private plaintiffs can't sue."

https://apnews.com/article/voting-rights-federal-court-private-lawsu its-00b9c4bb2174aa8077db296c3edf7c79?user_email=ac0c867de6e 83eb23515fd8f06cd2430d3a2cf96f5dcd56d9c00d48fff4dc30d&utm_ medium=Morning_Wire&utm_source=Sailthru&utm_campaign=Morn ing%20Wire%20Nov%2021%202023&utm_term=Morning%20W ire%20Subscribers

"Federal appeals court ruling threatens enforcement of the Voting Rights Act." www.politico.com/news/2023/11/20/federal-court-deals-devastating-blow-to-voting-rights-act-00128069#:~:text=A%20fede ral%20appeals%20court%20issued,the%20landmark%20civil%20rig hts%20law.

1 Grassroots Organizations and Educational Engagement

The Emergence of Dominican Americans in the U.S. Electoral Arena

This chapter examines the early incorporation of Dominicans and Dominican Americans into U.S. electoral politics in the 1980s and 1990s. I employ the demonyms "Dominicans" and "Dominican Americans" to refer to new immigrants from the Dominican Republic and long-standing immigrants or individuals of Dominican descent born in the United States, respectively. Also, I indistinctively use the demonym "Dominican Americans" for both groups as a means to advocate for the right of individuals of Dominican descent in the United States to claim their Dominican American identity irrespectively of their time of residence or citizenship status. As examined in this chapter, the 1980s were characterized by the prevalence of entrenched nationalistic ideas among some Dominican community leaders in the United States regarding the preservation of Dominican national identity by Dominican immigrants through the nurturing of links with politicians in the homeland, even at the expense of losing opportunities for political empowerment in the United States, an ideal that gradually dwindled in the 1990s with the ascent of Dominican American leaders to the U.S. electoral arena. The early incorporation of Dominican Americans into U.S. politics in the 1980s–1990s was preceded by the international political activism of Dominican exiles that started in 1916 against the first U.S. military occupation of the Dominican Republic and went on from the 1930s throughout the 1970s against the authoritarian regimes of Rafael Trujillo (1930–1961) and Joaquín Balaguer (1966–1978) and other dictatorships throughout Latin America and the Caribbean. This allowed the development of firm links between the Dominican Revolutionary Party (i.e., Partido Revolucionario Dominicano—PRD), founded in Cuba

DOI: 10.4324/9781003497455-2

in 1939, and Dominican exiles in the United States, particularly following the establishment of a PRD branch in New York City in the early 1940s. This development prompted a persistent collaboration between Dominican American politicians and their counterparts in the Dominican Republic, as other Dominican political parties, including the leftist Dominican Workers Party (i.e., Partido de los Trabajadores Dominicanos—PTD), opened branches in the United States as well, particularly starting in the 1960s.

Employing archival material and secondary sources, this chapter argues that the lack of U.S. citizenship (or legal status) hampered the possibilities of Dominican Americans to engage in electoral participation and representation. Instead, they joined grassroots and institutional organizations such as Area Policy Boards (APBs) and Community School Boards (CSBs) as a means to develop political empowerment. This strategy resulted in the emergence of young leaders who eventually became ethnic representatives of their communities at the municipal level and enforced a redistricting process that, in turn, allowed for the emergence of a Dominican American political enclave in New York City linked to the Democratic Party. Moreover, as in the case of other Latino/a/x immigrant groups, the alliances that Dominican Americans forged with other ethnic minorities such as Puerto Ricans and African Americans—contributed to the achievement of their political goals. Finally, I analyze the demographics and socioeconomic development of Dominican Americans during that time period in order to discern trends related to their rise to political prominence.

Dominican Exiles in the United States and Their Anti-Authoritarian Political Struggles

Dominican exiles in the United States played a prominent role in political crusades against the U.S. military occupations of the Dominican Republic (in 1916–1924 and 1965–1966, respectively) and the Trujillo (1930–1961) and Balaguer (1966–1978) dictatorships by joining international anti-occupation and anti-authoritarian movements that included militants from other Latin American and Caribbean countries. The history of Dominican exiles in the United States goes back to 1916–1924 during the first U.S. military occupation of the Dominican Republic. The U.S. occupation forces founded a Dominican National Guard, trained Trujillo, and later on supported the establishment of his long-standing autocratic regime. At the time, Dominican exiles settled in New York City and founded the Dominican Nationalist Commission (i.e., Comisión Nacionalista Dominicana) to protest against the occupation of their country and advocate for the restoration of Dominican sovereignty. The following wave of Dominican exiles arrived in New York City from the 1930s through the 1960s, a period in which a group of Dominican exiles (led by Angel Morales) founded the Dominican Patriotic Union (i.e., Unión Patriótica Dominicana) (Novas 2018).

Dominican exiles in New York City were exposed to the criminal actions of the Trujilloist intelligence services, as well as the attacks of racist gangs in the city due to the high level of racial segregation in the United States at that time. The exiles organized pickets during the dictator's visit to New York in 1939 and influenced public opinion regarding the situation of the Dominican Republic and its relationship with the United States. For example, they spread the idea that the John F. Kennedy administration had been involved in the murder of Trujillo in 1961. The exiles shuttled information from New York City to Washington, D.C., as well as Cuba, Puerto Rico, and Venezuela, where anti-Trujillo militants had also settled—although on a temporary basis due to their frequent relocation to other places (Atanay 1992).

In the 1940s, Dominican exiles in the United States and other Central American and Caribbean exiles joined the so-called "Caribbean Legion," also known as "the Legion" (i.e., Legión del Caribe), a military organization that fought against the Somoza and Trujillo dictatorships. The Legion also got involved in the Costa Rican civil war of 1948 that led to the presidency of José Figueres, with Dominican exiles Horacio Ornes and Juan Rodríguez becoming leading participants in the conflict (Ferrero 2016).

The main political party opposing Trujillo in exile was the Dominican Revolutionary Party (i.e., Partido Revolucionario Dominicano, or PRD), a progressive organization founded by Juan Bosch, Juan Isidro Jimenes Grullón, Angel Miolán, Nicolás Silfa, Virgilio Mainardi Reyna, and other exiles in Havana (Cuba) in 1939, with branches in Venezuela, Costa Rica, and the United States, as well as delegations in Puerto Rico, Panamá, Curaçao, and Aruba. The PRD went on to become the primary opposition party in the Dominican Republic after the breakdown of Trujillo regime, winning the presidency with Juan Bosch in 1962. In addition, the historic link of Dominican exiles in the United States with the Dominican Republic's

PRD created the conditions to develop strong ties between the PRD and Dominican American politicians collaborating in the strategic and financial sponsorship of electoral campaigns in the Dominican Republic and the United States, a tradition that was later followed by other major Dominican parties such as Balaguer's Reformist Party/ Reformist Social Christian Party (i.e., Partido Reformista/Partido Reformista Social Cristiano—PR/PRSC), and Bosch's Dominican Liberation Party (i.e., Partido de la Liberación Dominicana—PLD), as well as minor leftist parties such as the Dominican Workers Party (i.e., Partido de los Trabajadores Dominicanos—PTD). Those parties set up offices in the United States that supported the political activities of both Dominican and Dominican American candidates.

From the 1930s through the 1950s, Dominican exiles organized violent and nonviolent resistance actions against Trujillo. Yangling (2013) states that in 1946, exile leaders led by Juan Bosch planned a coup d'état against Trujillo, and the PRD's branch in New York stockpiled weapons and supplies in the homes of Dominican exiles living in Manhattan. In addition, it was a common practice for Dominican exiles to buy surplus World War II weapons in the United States and smuggle arms and operatives and hide them throughout Florida as part of anti-Trujillo military operations. Yangling (2013, 47) also highlights the gender inclusivity prevailing among Dominican exiles during the Trujillo era. Opposing the objectification of women by the ruthless dictator, the Dominican exile movement allowed for the integration of women as equal players, co-conspirators, and decision makers, as epitomized in the decentralized political style of the PRD that favored the integration of grassroots organizations and open debate as part of its democratic decision-making process.

Ironically, while Dominican exiles fought against Trujillo, the autocrat presented his regime as a panacea to European Jewish refugees who survived the horrors of the Nazi regime. The participation of Trujillo's diplomats in the Évian Conference in 1939 led to the regime's offer to settle 100,000 Jewish refugees in the Dominican Republic. Nevertheless, the agreement between the Dominican Republic's government and representatives of the Jewish community resulted in the arrival of a mere 645 Jews from 1938 to 1945, despite the issuing of 5,000 Dominican visas to European Jews during that period. The Jewish refugees settled in Sosúa, Puerto Plata, with the strategic and financial support of the American Jewish Distribution Committee, that established the Dominican Republic Settlement

Association (DORSA), but many in the small refugee population did not adapt to the island (and its political climate) and left following the end of World War II (Novas 2018, Holocaust Sources in Context). In addition, Trujillo welcomed 3,000 Communist refugees from Spain, a strategic decision that has been interpreted by some scholars as a means for Trujillo to increase the White population of the Dominican Republic (as was the case with the Jewish refugees), provide a democratic veneer to his dictatorship, and create a praetorian guard of foreign loyal acolytes while assuring the support of the United States as its main ally in the anti-Communist geostrategic politics of the Caribbean. Indeed, many of the Communist refugees from Spain were victimized by the regime and forced to seek asylum in other countries. By 1944, only 800 remained in the country. Among the Spanish refugees in the Dominican Republic was Jesús de Galíndez, who worked in several administrative positions for Trujillo, including the Secretaryships of Labor and Foreign Relations. Galíndez was also serving the U.S. government as a Central Intelligence Agency (CIA) informant and as Federal Bureau of Investigation (FBI) *agent Rojas (NY-507S)*, providing information to the United States about the activities of Spanish, Dominican, and Puerto Rican Communists and Spanish Falangists in the Dominican Republic. Galíndez eventually fled the regime's terror and migrated to the United States in 1946, where he was abducted and murdered by Trujillo's intelligence services (with the support of the CIA and the FBI) in 1956, right after writing his doctoral dissertation at Columbia University about Trujillo's brutal tyranny (Manuel de Dios Unanue1999; Vega 1984; Block 1989; Dana 1992; Jiménez Polanco 1999b, 94; Mota Zurdo 2020).

In the post-World War II era, Dominican exiles joined an international anti-authoritarian movement made up by democratic leaders from Latin America, including Cuban reformists, Venezuelan democrats, and Mexican labor leaders (Yangling 2013). Leftist media outlets such as *The Militant*, the organ of the U.S. Socialist Workers Party (SWP), recount the activities of Dominican exiles, among them, Octavio E. Moscoso, a medical doctor with a Ph.D. in Spanish literature from Columbia University. Moscoso initially opposed the 1916–1924 U.S. occupation of the Dominican Republic. Later on, he became a fervent opponent to Rafael Trujillo's regime while he was living in the United States and was sentenced to thirty-year imprisonment in absentia, which forced him to live in exile. He was a Dominican nationalist and a revolutionary socialist, as well as a sympathizer of the U.S. Socialist Worker Party. He was widely known in Latin American political circles due to his interest on the region's affairs (Ring 1966).

On April 15, 1962, almost one year after the assassination of dictator Trujillo, the Organization for the Return of Anti-Trujillo Exiles, led by Roberto Sánchez, Lydia Castro, and Dylce Grullón Vda. Álvarez signed a petition in New York City to demand the right for all of the Trujillo regime exiles to return to the Dominican Republic. *The Militant* denounced that U.S. authorities refused to allow some anti-Trujillo exiles to embark for their homeland and labeled it as a blatant interference in the internal affairs of the Dominican Republic. In addition, some exiles who managed to travel to the Dominican Republic were not allowed to enter the country on the grounds of their professed beliefs. The journal alleges that the Dominican Republic's Council of State feared the return of exiles because "veiled Trujilloism" prevailed in the new administration, and according to *The Miami Herald*, members of the administration were running multi-million-dollar businesses and properties that had belonged to the Trujillo family (The Militant 1962).

On April 24, 1966, the Dominican Constitutionalist Front and the New York chapter of the Puerto Rico Independence Movement sponsored a rally in New York City, in which approximately 300 persons, mostly Dominicans and Puerto Ricans, marched to express solidarity with the struggle of the people in the Dominican Republic and to demand the withdrawal of U.S. occupation troops from the country. The demonstration was part of an international Dominican solidarity week called by the Tricontinental Conference held in Cuba earlier that year (The Militant 1966).

In the 1970s, the media outlet *Palante* of the Puerto Rican Revolutionary Labor Organization (i.e., Organización Obrera Revolucionaria Puertorriqueña), a member of the Young Lords Party, informed that hundreds of Dominicans in New York marched against the repressive regime of Balaguer and its violent actions against dissidents. They also marched in support of Francisco Caamaño's revolutionary military movement for the liberation of the Dominican Republic from Balaguer's authoritarian regime (Palante 1973).

As previously analyzed, Dominicans who immigrated to the United States as political exiles from the 1940s through the 1970s mostly settled in New York City and were involved in political activities whose main goal was to overturn the Trujillo and Balaguer regimes, as well as other Latin American and Caribbean dictatorships. The political activities of exiles, that started with the PRD in the 1940s, and continued with both the PRD and the PTD in the 1960s and 1970s, served as a catalyst to further political mobilizations among Dominican Americans activists. In addition, during the 1980s and 1990s migratory waves, that coincided with the democratizing process in the Dominican Republic, former exiles joined younger Dominican American activists to participate in the U.S. domestic politics through grassroots institutions and electoral campaigns. Some of them continued to nurture tight links with political parties in the Dominican Republic while directing their activities toward electoral competition in the United States. In addition, former political exiles of the 1965 post-civil war era joined labor unions in the United States.[1]

Community Activism and Electoral Competition in the 1980s and 1990s

The early access of Dominican Americans to the politics of empowerment in the United States started in the 1980s through the creation of grassroots organizations such as cultural and sport clubs and professional associations addressed at gaining labor opportunities. This strategy allowed the Dominican American community in New York City to elect its first members to the Area Policy Boards (APBs) and Community School Boards (CSBs) in Washington Heights.

During the 1980s, half of the documented Latino/a/x immigrants in New York State were Dominicans and Dominican Americans with an average of over 15,000 from 1983 to 1989 (Larancuent, Alvarez-Lopez, and Mejia 1991, 5–6). At the time, Dominican Americans represented a very small constituency within the U.S. national electorate, which was controlled by Republicans for over a decade under Presidents Ronald Reagan (1981–1989) and George H. W. Bush (1989–1993), followed by a Democratic eight-year reign under Pres. Bill Clinton (1993–2001).

For over a decade (1970s–1980s), María Luna, the first Dominican female district leader, held her position at Upper Manhattan's Assembly District No. 71 with the support of the Democratic Party machinery. In 1985, the Dominican American community in New York City elected Julio Hernández as the first male district leader of Dominican descent who won the position without the backing of the Democratic Party (Jordan 1997; Torres-Saillant and Hernández 1998). Hernández was a long-term community activist who worked to empower Dominicans through the acquisition of U.S. citizenship status, something that was criticized by nationalist members of the community, who argued that it would eventually weaken the relationship of Dominican immigrants with politicians in the Dominican Republic.[2] Hernández defeated incumbent Dr. Albert Bloomberg, an emeritus professor at Rutgers University. Hernández later relinquished his seat to Dominican Sixto Medina, and in 1992, he unsuccessfully ran as candidate to the New York State Assembly for District 72 (Alduey Sierra 1992; Lescaille 1992, 4).

In 1985, the Dominican Political Front was founded as a grassroots movement addressed at gaining the representation of Dominicans and Dominican Americans in New York City's anti-poverty agencies such as the Community Development Agency (CDA) and its locally elected advisory groups, known as Area Policy Boards (APBs), that controlled the flow of economic resources to the community and allowed the participation of non-U.S. citizens. The Front achieved the election of eight Dominican leaders to the Area Policy Boards, and although the APBs were eliminated in the late 1980s, they proved to be a crucial step in the emergence of Dominican American electoral empowerment.

The Front also challenged the political establishment of the Democratic Party in the Washington Heights and Inwood neighborhoods during the election of community leader Julio Hernández as the first Dominican male district leader. Hernández was backed up by the Front to challenge the first Dominican female district leader in New York City, Maria Luna, a devoted community advocate who had been reelected to that position for over a decade through the support of the Democratic machinery, and who in the early 1990s raised her voice for the redistricting process. Moreover, Ivelisse Fairchild and Sixto Medina were also elected as Dominican district leaders for the Democratic Party (Lescaille 1992; Jordan 1997). In addition, the Community Association of Progressive Dominicans (*Asociación Comunitaria de Dominicanos Progresistas*, or CAPD) was founded in the mid-1980s to work in defense of the representation of Dominican parents at the Community School Boards (CSBs).[3]

In the early 1990s, the Dominican leadership in New York City was concentrated in four major organizations that recognized the importance of education in the development of political empowerment: the

Northern Manhattan Coalition for Immigrant Rights (NMCIR), the Community Association of Progressive Dominicans (CAPD), Alianza Dominicana, and Latinos United for Political Action (LUPA) (Lescaille 1992; Jordan 1997). These organizations joined Latino/a/x parents in the creation of a multiethnic movement that supported the election of several Dominican activists to the Community School Board No. 6, including Guillermo Linares and Apolinar Trinidad. As stated by Lescaille (1992, 3):

> The boards [Community School Boards] were seen as electoral mechanisms to address school overcrowding and substandard education. The organizations and parents exposed the educational mismanagement, corruption, and political patronage that had detrimentally impacted Dominican children in the school system.

In his analysis of the role played by the Community School Boards in the development of the Dominican political empowerment in New York City, Anthony Stevens-Acevedo has pointed out that:

> The Community School Boards were represented by immigrant working parents who seized significant local power. Some of them were Dominicans who had done activism in the Dominican Republic or had completed their formal education before arriving in the United States. The CSB system was the only space where Dominican immigrants developed leadership in an institution. This allowed the emergence of a Dominican community leadership that created the conditions for the subsequent emergence of an electoral leadership. Indeed, the CSBs were a training space for many Dominican activists who later on became political leaders. At the end of the 1990s, the CSBs turned into a mechanism of direct citizenry participation in which almost everybody could participate in decisions that were essential in the use of important public resources. It was a revendicating and militancy space in which many debates intersecting ethnic and racial issues were held. I was a member of the Community Action Movement for Education – CAFE (i.e., Movimiento Acción Comunal para la Educación) and vividly recall the active role of Nilma Báez, Felicia Peguero, Yolanda Pineda, and Marcos Navarro in the enhancement of the school system through the CSBs.[4]

The Community School Boards ran public schools from kindergarten through junior high schools. Their members were elected through a democratic process that allowed for the participation of both U.S. citizen and non-U.S. citizen parents. This prompted the engagement of many Dominican immigrants who demanded the improvement of school infrastructure, teaching, and academic programs. For example, the Dominican American community leader and schoolteacher Anthony Stevens-Acevedo denounced the lack of space, teachers, security, academic, recreational and artistic programs, and the poor communication between the administration and parents, as well as the lack of respect for the cultural background of the children in Community School Board No. 6 (Stevens-Acevedo 1993a). He rejected the traditional ethnic classification of CSB No. 6 inherent in the use of the generic term "Hispanics," as it disregarded the concentration of specific national-origin groups, such as Dominicans, Puerto Ricans, Cubans, and Mexicans—among others. Stevens-Acevedo argued that the term "Hispanics" was not considered valid any longer due to the increasing multinational backgrounds of the students, parents, and employees. He also demanded employment opportunities for Dominicans in CSB No. 6, a demand that was widely supported by the Dominican members of CSB No. 6 (Stevens-Acevedo 1993c).

The struggle for access to political power in Community School Board No. 6 represented the first organized political movement toward increasing the electoral representation of Dominican Americans in New York City. As pointed out by Guillermo Linares, Dominican community leaders in Washington Heights mobilized over 10,000 parents for the school elections in 1985, which represented half of the registered parents in the entire city (Viñuales 1997). The massive mobilization and the criticism of Dominican organizations and community leaders of the New York City school system encountered the rejection of conservative White, Jewish, African American, and Puerto Rican leaders who saw the emerging political empowerment of Dominicans as a threat to their persistent control of the CSBs. The booming democratic activism of Dominicans generated an atmosphere of constant confrontations with conservative sectors who typified the former as noisy, defiant, and insurgent Communists (as there were some Leftist leaders, including former exiles who had participated in the 1965 civil war or "Revolución de Abril") who wanted to take control over the CSBs. Stevens-Acevedo asserts that an arduous campaign of a presumed atmosphere of corruption and lack of prestige in the CSBs was purposefully sparked by conservative Republicans and Democrats, which ultimately led to the elimination of Community School Board No. 6 by Puerto Rican Chancellor Nathan Quiñones in 1987.[5] This setback, nevertheless, did not discourage Dominican activists to persist in their struggle to demand the application of affirmative action initiatives for minority students and the nomination of Dominicans to school posts and Community School Boards (Lescaille 1992, 3). But the removal of CSB No. 6 was subsequently followed by the further eradication of the entire Community School Board system as a unique space of open participation and the reestablishment of the old hierarchical and non-participatory school system.[6]

The elimination of the Community School Board system was in essence prompted by the fear of conservative political sectors to the emerging empowerment of Dominican Americans and the threat that they could purportedly pose to the establishment, something that is typical of ethnic and racial politics: whenever an ethnic or racial minority group is emerging, there are obstacles created from the top of the system to avoid that they become "so strong" as to challenge the power of the traditional White elite. Therefore, the divide and conquer strategy operates as a dissuasive mechanism spread by the elite among ethnic minorities, implying that those who came first should avoid at any cost that new communities take over their meager portion of the political cake, which results in fiery confrontations that only benefit the White dominant group.

Therefore, the emerging empowerment of the Dominican American community came at a high cost, but its work bore fruit, and as a result of its leaders' participation in the Community School Boards, its representation in New York City electoral politics gradually increased in the 1990s with the election of Guillermo Linares as the first Dominican American councilmember in New York City District No. 10 in 1991. That same year, Key Palacios, daughter of the anti-Trujillo exile Juan M. Díaz, was elected as the first female Dominican American councilmember in Englewood Cliffs, New Jersey. The Dominican American candidates to the 1991 New York City Council position were María Luna, Guillermo Linares, and Adriano Espaillat. Luna was former chair of the local Community Board No. 12 and was embedded in the Democratic machine politics since she became involved in the Audubon Reform Democratic Club in 1983 (Batista 1991).

Linares occupied the position of councilmember from 1992 through 2001, and nine years later (2010), he was elected as a member of the New York State Assembly for district 72, representing Washington Heights. In the interim, Linares was appointed as Commissioner of the Mayor's Office of Immigrant Affairs (2004–2009).

Espaillat, who began his gradual ascent into the U.S. political establishment in the 1990s, was Linares' sturdiest rival and the man who would lead the top political representation of Dominican Americans in the U.S. electoral realm in the forthcoming three decades. After winning the Democratic district leader seat No. 12 in 1994, Espaillat's political career started to rise consistently and he became the first Dominican American to win a New York State Assembly seat in the election for district No. 72 in 1996, a position that he occupied from 1997 to 2010. In addition, he occupied the post of New York state senator representing Democratic district No. 31 from 2011 to 2016. Finally, in 2016, he was elected as a member of the U.S. House of Representatives for New York's district No. 13 and has been reelected ever since.

The electoral victories for Dominican Americans in the 1980s–1990s took place following decades of growing political action through educational, professional, social, and cultural engagement. Of particular importance was their active leadership in Area Policy Boards, Community School Boards, and grassroots organizations in Washington Heights and Inwood, two neighborhoods in the northernmost part of Manhattan that concentrated the largest number of Dominican Americans in New York City.

Linares was a teacher and a parent with children attending New York City public schools, which allowed him to engage in social activism in Community School Boards and gradually develop a political leadership. He played an active role in Community School Board No. 6 by advocating for the building of public schools to serve the growing immigrant community in Washington Heights. Also, as a CUNY student, he was involved in a movement against the elimination of free tuition. In addition, he helped to establish the Community Association of Progressive Dominicans, the Puerto Rican/Latino Education Round Table, and the Parents Coalition for Education in New York City. He was also instrumental in the founding of the CUNY Dominican Studies Institute at City College, the Audubon Partnership for Economic Development, and the Center for Latin American and Latino Studies at the CUNY Graduate Center (Stevens-Acevedo 1991).

Espaillat's background in community services includes his membership in the executive board of Community School Board No. 12 and his leadership in the Washington Heights Victim Services Community Office and in the Washington Senior Center Board of Directors. In addition, he was president of the 34th Precinct Community Council and a founding member of the Northern Manhattan Democrats for Change and of Governor Mario Cuomo's Dominican Advisory Board. His electoral campaign for district leader was endorsed by Dominican community organizations and business leaders, as well as politicians from diverse ethnic groups, such as Puerto Rican assemblyman Roberto Ramirez, councilman Jose Rivera, district leader William Alicea, African American assemblyman Keith Wright, and Italian American assemblyman Vito Lopez, as well as female district leader Ivy Fairchild. Espaillat was also elected with the endorsement of the African American candidate to the New York City Mayoral Office David N. Dinkins, who had hired Dominican Zenaida Méndez as the representative to the office of Hispanic issues (Guillén 1990b).

Redistricting and the Rise of Linares and Espaillat in New York Politics

The election of Linares as the first Dominican-born New York City councilmember for District 10 was the result of the implementation in 1990 of a new City Charter that effected the redrawing of New York City's electoral maps and the creation of a Dominican-majority City Council district. A revision of the City Charter for New York required that the City Council be expanded to reduce the size of districts and provide opportunities for the election of minority candidates. This revision forced the redrawing of all districts and required that the city implement the fair and effective representation of racial and language minority groups protected under the Voting Rights Act of 1965. It further required that voting block neighborhoods be redistricted every ten years after the national census had taken place, giving preference to racial and ethnic group concentrations, often termed as "majority-minority districts." The New York City Districting Commission (NYCDC) completed the redesign of new districts by mid-1991 and new City Council elections took place in the fall of that year. As detailed in a NYCDC report, it held public hearings to reach out to historically excluded groups, such as the Dominican community (Graham 1996, 108–109). As pointed out by Stevens Acevedo (2023), the creation of new districts through the fragmentation of old districts increases the possibilities of ethnic and racial minorities (i.e., Dominicans) to gain electoral representation. Moreover, the revision of districts every ten years, following the results of the census, promotes more equitable representation.

Indeed, the creation of District 10 in Washington Heights as a Dominican-based councilmanic district was crucial for the improvement of the socioeconomic conditions of the Dominican American community, as the City Council is the organization in charge of proposing and approving the city budget together with the mayor's office. Moreover, the City Council is the branch that has the most extensive contact with the community and represents its interests most directly (Larancuent, Alvarez-Lopez, and Mejia 1991, 7).

As pointed out by Pessar (1995, 73), the U.S. redistricting process was a "by-product of federal legislation directed at redressing the old practice of dividing geographic concentrations of ethnic groups into many districts to dilute their influence." Therefore, in New York City, as in other communities throughout the United States, representatives of racial and ethnic minorities proposed alternative plans for electoral districts to eradicate such disenfranchisement.

In effect, territorial and demographic considerations were included in the proposals presented to the NYCDC by Dominican American activists who were advocating for redistricting. Among the activists were members of the Northern Manhattan Committee for Fair Representation (NMCFR), many of whom had already served in public office and counted with the support of African Americans, Puerto Ricans, and Whites. The NMCFR lobbied for the creation of a district that could be won by a Dominican, something that was clearly expressed in its proposals to the NYCDC in which its members said that they were seeking for "the creation of a Dominican-based councilmanic district, that coinciding with a massive voter registration campaign would maximize Dominican political potential at the polls" (Graham 1996, 111).

The NMCFR identified itself as an "ethnically diverse, nonpartisan group of persons who live and/or work in the areas of Hamilton Heights, Washington Heights, Inwood, and Marble Hill." Its purpose was to help the community, especially the underserved Hispanic population, attain a fairer, more equitable representation in elective public office to which it was fully entitled by reason of its numbers and its needs. The NMCFR believed that such representation was essential to make real progress in solving the oppressive problems that plagued the area, including the lack of decent jobs, the intolerable overcrowding of schools and homes, the pervasive death-dealing traffic in drugs, and the woeful inadequacies in accessible and affordable health care services (The Washington Heights Citizen & The Inwood News 1991).

Representatives of the NMCFR believed in the viability of the new district in Northern Manhattan in which the Dominican American community could elect a candidate of its choice. In their proposals, they emphasized the importance of the large concentration of Dominicans in Washington Heights, their political cohesion denoted in the great strides made in the Community School Boards, and their economic investments in the area (Pessar 1995, 74). The NMCFR proposed that the new district would use Broadway as its western border and would reach from 158th Street to the northern end of Manhattan and run east to the Harlem River.

A study conducted by Dominican activists from the Centro de Estudios Dominicanos indicated that the ethnic composition of District 10 in 1991 was: 53% Dominicans, 13% Puerto Ricans, 6% Cubans, 9% African Americans, 9% Whites, and 10% others. Most of the interviewees said that they would vote for a Dominican candidate, but the campaigning work was intensive as the number of registered Latino/a/x voters was low and many of them did not know their candidates (Larancuent, Alvarez-Lopez and Mejia 1991, 13, 16). As pointed out by Graham (1996, 111), the ethnic composition of registered voters in District 10 was 44% Hispanic (of a total 78% of Hispanic residents) and approximately 10% African Americans and Whites, respectively.

During the electoral campaign, Dominicans strengthened their national identity while relying on the support of Puerto Rican elected officials who were looking to increase the number of Latino/a/x districts in the city (Lescaille 1992; Jordan 1997). Prominent among them was Congressmember José E. Serrano, who stated that Dominicans constituted a force that had achieved enough economic, political, and social development to gain representation at the municipal and federal levels (Guillén 1990a).

In his campaign for councilmember, Linares used the bilingual slogan "When he wins, we win" (*Cuando gana él, ganamos todos*) and "When he wins, our kids win" ("*Cuando gana él, nuestros niños ganan*"). He proposed training Washington Heights and Inwood community groups to promote the wellbeing and improvement of the quality of life of residents by teaching them mechanisms for political participation in governmental institutions and for claiming their rights and access to resources from those institutions. In this context, he anticipated the identification and promotion of local leaders, particularly youth, and informational methods to help the blooming entrepreneurial sector tap into local financial aid offered by the city to ethnic minority businesses (Anthony Stevens-Acevedo 1992a).

In addition, Linares proposed to create English language programs that fueled the strengthening of human capital through the access of residents to competitive jobs and professional achievements. The main social issues covered in his campaign program were the improvement of affordability and quality of rent and housing, the availability of health care centers and doctors, more assistance and funds for the elderly population, the creation of childcare centers, English classes and accessible services for immigrants, the construction of new school buildings, the development of after-school programs, and increasing school retention and the participation of parents in school activities. Linares also wanted to reduce violence (mostly associated to drug and gun trafficking), marginality, unemployment, and poverty. In this context, he advocated for the passing of laws to punish drug and gun trafficking and increase police patrolling.

Linares emphasized the importance of recognizing and respecting the multiethnic composition of Washington Heights and Inwood, in which the larger Dominican community coexisted with other Latino/a/x groups, as well as Jews, African Americans, and Anglos, among others. He recommended that in order to achieve these goals the city should assign financial resources for cultural community activities.

Following his electoral triumph, Linares expressed his satisfaction for having run what he called "a grassroots campaign" in which half of the contributions were in the amount of $25.00 dollars or less, oftentimes raised at house parties in his supporters' living rooms, where he met voters and answered their questions. Linares raised a total of $40,011 in campaign funds, whereas his main contender Adriano Espaillat raised just $29,978, and others like Maria Luna and Harry Fotopoulos raised $9,195 and $200, respectively (Stevens-Acevedo 1991).

During his tenure as councilmember, Linares' political power was challenged by Adriano Espaillat's leadership, but the fierce competition between the two gradually faded away as the years went by as

Espaillat's political strength outgrew Linares' after the former became the first Dominican American elected as state assemblymember in 1996, and then winning reelection seven times without counting on Linares's support during any of those terms.

Espaillat launched his campaign for New York State Assembly district 72 in the George Washington High School's area, and in his speech, he stated that his candidacy represented "a change in the political leadership," as he had the same cultural and social background as his Washington Heights constituents, a veiled reference to Assemblymember Brian Murtaugh's Irish American origin. Espaillat stated that he expected that Dominicans, who made up the "soul and the heart of the community," had for once and all an assemblyman that knew their real needs, and who claimed and enforced their rights (Butten 1996a). Espaillat competed in a hard-fought electoral contest to dismantle Murtaugh's entrenched power after the latter's tenure in office for the previous sixteen years. He stated that he was confronting "a powerful machinery" that did not want to allow change. Espaillat expected a majoritarian Dominican American and Hispanic vote following what he called "the new citizenship boom" during which many Latino/a/x people would register to vote to push for political change. With his campaign slogan "All for Espaillat" (*Todos por Espaillat*), he expected to count on the support of Cubans, Puerto Ricans, Irish, African Americans, Jews, and White Americans, including politicians, businesspeople, entrepreneurs, community leaders, and union members. Murtaugh, in turn, relied on the support of several prominent political leaders, including Dominican American Guillermo Linares and Isabel Evangelista, Olga Méndez (the first Puerto Rican woman elected to a state legislature), Puerto Rican Fernando Ferrer (borough president of the Bronx from 1987 to 2001), and African American Charles Rangel (U.S. representative in New York City from 1971 to 2017).

Espaillat devoted his political work as a Democratic New York State assemblymember to achieve immigrant family reunification, the creation of childcare centers, the reform of bilingual education, and the improvement of public schools (particularly George Washington High School in Washington Heights with a student body that was 80% Dominican American) and public transportation, and increasing health care coverage. In addition, Espaillat signed with Governor George Pataki a compensation law to benefit the relatives of a murdered taxi driver. He also participated in the discussion of topics related to technology, the economy, and the natural environment. In an interview, Espaillat emphasized the importance of investing in education and stated:

> Our future as a community relies on the educational level of our children, the quality of education, the kind of education that they receive, and how they will be able to compete for good jobs in the future.
>
> (Dominguez 2001)

Linares' support for the reelection of Irish American John Brian Murtaugh was considered by some activists as an act of treason toward the Dominican community (Guillén 1992). Murtaugh, a conservative Democratic state assemblyman who represented districts 73 and 72, respectively (1981–1982, 1983–1996), was against multiethnic representation in the CSBs and the emerging political empowerment of Dominican Americans, getting to the point of disputing their candidacies in the election for CSB No. 6, which provoked the reaction of several community sectors who publicly expressed their indignation against him (Stevens-Acevedo 1993a, 1993b).

But this was not the only time that Linares and Espaillat tested their political muscle in their fight for building their own Dominican ethnic faction within the Democratic Party, something that was seen by some analysts as a negative element of ethnic politics (Ricourt 2002), but that I view as a positive component of democratic political competition in which dissention can enlarge the constituents' political choices and the quality of the candidates' electoral programs. The particularity was that—on this occasion—Linares was backing a non-Dominican American candidate against Espaillat, which affected the possibility of increasing Dominican American electoral representation at a critical moment for this emerging ethnic political community, something that was vigorously rejected by some groups. Afterward, Linares changed his strategy and decided to continue his opposition to Espaillat by supporting Dominican American candidates. Indeed, in 1998, during Espaillat's campaign for reelection to the New York State Assembly, Linares backed Víctor Morrisette-Romero against him, while Espaillat had previously supported Roberto Lizardo against Linares in the Democratic primary for the City Council. Espaillat stated that he had sought meetings with Linares to address their differences, but to no avail. And then, he added: "Politics is about sharing and about consensus, but when someone is not able to share and to follow and is only willing to lead, there will be difficulties" (Hicks 1998a). Espaillat also asserted that there was a history of political hostility against him, and this round was only a new stage that was not going to prosper. Linares, in turn, pointed out that, in any case, a Dominican would keep the position (Viñuales 1998).

The other Dominican American candidate who disputed Espaillat's seat during his reelection campaign for the State Assembly was Isabel Evangelista, a female Dominican district leader and educator, and a member of the political club Concerned Democratic Coalition of Northern Manhattan who was an ally of Linares and Morrisette-Romero. Evangelista, who was a former tenant organizer, claimed that Espaillat was tied to the landlords' interests who supported his campaign in 1996 during the New York State Assembly race. Evangelista's argument was seconded by Morrisette-Romero, who stated that Espaillat had received support from landlords and had abandoned the interests of tenants (Hicks 1998a). Evangelista attested that Espaillat had received tens of thousands of dollars in contributions from landlords. But Espaillat rejected Evangelista's charges stating that they formed part of an old argument used to misinform his constituents and that her candidacy was a response to the blind ambition of Councilman Linares. He acknowledged that he received a contribution from an organization of landlords, but it was far less than the tens of thousands of dollars cited by his opponent. He sustained that he voted for the extension of rent controls until 2003, and that he would vote again to extend it or make it permanent. Hicks (1998b) pointed out that, according to campaign records, Espaillat received over $5,000 from two landlord groups, as well as other donations in thousands of dollars from several individual contributors related to the real estate business.

Demography and the Socioeconomic Development of Dominican Americans in the 1980s–1990s

The embryonic engagement of Dominican Americans in U.S. electoral politics in the 1980s and early 1990s was prompted by the growing number of people of Dominican descent in the country, due primarily to massive immigration from the Dominican Republic. The Immigration and Naturalization Service (INS) documented the arrival of 226,853 Dominicans in the United States as permanent residents from 1982 to 1989. In addition, Dominicans outnumbered all other immigrant applicants for U.S. citizenship (i.e., naturalization) during that same time period (Lescaille 1992; Jordan 1997). The largest concentration of Dominicans in the United States resided in New York City, specifically in Manhattan. In 1990, Dominicans represented the second largest Latino/a/x group in New York City with 332,713 residents, behind Puerto Ricans with 896,763 residents, but the expectation was that Dominicans would become the largest ethnic group in New York City within the next ten years. According to official figures, the Dominican-origin population in the United States rose from 170,817 in 1980 to 511,297 in 1990; of which 357,868 resided in New York State, 52,807 in New Jersey, 34,268 in Florida, 30,177 in Massachusetts, 9,374 in Rhode Island, 3,687 in Pennsylvania, and 3,946 in Connecticut. The largest concentration of Dominicans was in New York City with 332,713 Dominicans, of which 136,696 (41.1%) were living in Manhattan, 87,261 (26.2%) in the Bronx, 55,301 (16.6%) in Brooklyn, 52,309 (15.7%) in Queens, and 1,146 (0.4%) in Staten Island. The largest concentration of Dominicans in Manhattan was in the Washington Heights and Inwood neighborhoods with 86,273 residents (Stevens-Acevedo 1992b; Hernández and Rivera-Batiz 2003, 11–22).

At the socioeconomic level, Dominicans in New York City experienced low incomes and high levels of poverty. Data shows that in 1989, Dominican per capita household income in New York City was lower than for the overall Latino/a/x, Black, Asian, and White populations. Per capita household income for Dominicans was $8,659, compared to $11,515 for Latinos/as/xs, $14,573 for Blacks, $18,189 for Asians, and $31,026 for Whites. The poverty rate for Dominicans was 36.3%, whereas the overall poverty rate in New York City stood at 16.9%, which meant that one out of every three Dominicans lived in a household with income under the poverty line. As an ethnic minority population, Dominicans were greatly affected by the economic recession that took place from 1989 to 1993—considered the worst since the Great Depression of the 1930s. The economic downturn prompted the loss of hundreds of thousands of jobs in New York City (Hernández and Rivera-Batiz 2003, 28).

Hernández and Rivera-Batiz (2003, 28–29) analyze several factors contributing to the high poverty level of Dominicans in the 1990s, including age, gender and marital status, immigration, and labor market forces (e.g., unemployment and earnings). With regards to age, the authors assert that the average young age of Dominicans explains their lower income as labor market rewards are positively correlated with age, seniority, and work experience. The average age of the Dominican population was less than that of other groups in New York City; therefore, their average income was lower, and their poverty rates were higher. The overall Dominican population had a median age of about 30 years, which was substantially lower than the median age in the United States (at 35.4 years) and in New York City (at 34.4 years).

In relation to gender and marital status, Hernández and Rivera-Batiz (2003) argue that the comparatively high poverty level among Dominicans was due to families led by separated, divorced, and single women (with children) who received a lower income in the labor market as compared to married couple families. Dominican families headed by women with no spouse present accounted for 32.5% in the United States and 38.2% in New York City, compared to 13.3% for all female-headed households in the United States and 22.1% in New York City.

The large percentage of recently arrived Dominican immigrants was a major demographic force accounting for the high poverty rate among Dominicans in the United States and particularly New York City in the 1990s, due to the substantial income differences between recent immigrants and the rest of the population. The immigrant newcomers encountered difficulties entering the labor market as they adjusted to the U.S. economy and American society. For instance, the annual per capita household income of Dominicans who immigrated to the United States in 1999 was $9,377, compared to $12,556 for those who moved to the United States before 1990. In relation to the U.S. labor force, the authors show that the participation rate among Dominicans lies well below that of the overall population of the United States. It was approximately 64% for Dominican men compared to 72.7% for overall participation in the country's labor force, and 53.1% for Dominican women compared to 58.5% among non-Hispanic White women in 2000. The labor force participation of Dominicans in New York City was even lower: 60.9% for men and 49.1% for women, which may explain the comparatively lower income of Dominican New Yorkers. The labor force participation rate among Dominican New Yorkers declined from 75.6% in 1980 to 73.1% in 1990 (Hernández and Rivera-Batiz 2003).

Data on the educational attainment of Dominicans in New York City in 1980 and 1990 shows important progress among U.S.-born

Dominicans as 31.7% of them attained a college education in 1980 and 42.8% in 1990 (Hernández and Rivera-Batiz 2003, 54). These numbers inform us about the investment of Dominican Americans on human capital that, as we will see in the next chapter, persisted through years to come.

Political Challenges and Achievements in the 1990s

The ascent of Dominican Americans within New York City electoral politics took place amid a hostile economic environment affected by Mayor Dinkins' economic program addressed at achieving macro-economic stability by increasing direct taxes and reducing social expenditures in education, health, jobs, and social services (Sierra 1991). In addition, the social milieu in Washington Heights was plagued by a high level of violence expressed through police brutality, drug trafficking and drug use, racism, xenophobia, a lack of health care services, the poor quality of home heating services, workplace abuses, the displacement of small businesses, and an inefficient transportation system (Stevens-Acevedo 1992c).

Dominican local news in the United States reported that the statistics on crime in New York City included the violent death of 2,000 individuals in 1990. It also reported on the death of 500 Dominicans by the end of 1989, and 400 just in the spring of 1990—all linked to drug trafficking (Listín USA 1990–1991). In addition, the high rate of violent crimes affected *bodega* (grocery store) owners and gipsy cab drivers who were the victims of robberies, murders, and police harassment (Escotto 1990; Guillén 1990–1991). This widespread structural violence included the death of José (Kiko) García, killed by police officer Michael O'Keefe from the 34th Precinct, a police unit that was under investigation for its corruption and brutality. Kiko García's death provoked the reaction of hundreds of Dominicans who occupied the streets of Washington Heights and rioted for several days starting on July 3, 1992, after the brutal incident (WNBC/Channel 4 1992). What started as a peaceful demonstration led by Councilmember Linares to protest the shooting, turned into a violent riot following the speech of Mayor David N. Dinkins, resulting in another person being killed by the police. The media reported that the riot took place during a particular difficult time for Mayor Dinkins as it happened just a week before the Democratic National Convention, a period during which he had been trying to reassure the public that "his administration was committed to guaranteeing the integrity of the police force and moving forcefully to deal with charges of corruption and brutality" (Dao 1992).[7]

García's death brought together civic and business groups and political organizations that called for a thorough investigation into the killing and for more attention to the social problems of the Dominican community in Washington Heights. As stated by the head of New York City's Commission on Human Rights, Dennis DeLeon, Dominicans were considered as the most politicized community in the city. In a *New York Times* report, DeLeon expressed, "[T] there are more clubs per square inch in Washington Heights that you will find anywhere in the city. Dominicans brought a lot of the island politics with them, and that creates a structure for how they organize here" (Newman 1992).

The extent of tragic acts of violence also reached public schools, which sparked the broad mobilization of Dominican Americans in 1992 demanding the elimination of school violence, an increase in the quality of education, and the construction of three new high schools in Washington Heights. A rally was led by Councilmember Linares and thirteen community organizations, including the Dominican Youth Union (i.e., Unión de Jovenes Dominicanos, or UJD), the Dominican Women Caucus (i.e., Caucus de Mujeres Dominicanas), the Dominican Parade Committee (i.e., Comité del Desfile Dominicano), the George Washington Public School Parents Association (i.e., Asociación de Padres de la Escuela George Washington), the Northern Manhattan Partnership, the City College Student Government, the Hostos Community College Dominican Students Association, the Lehman College Dominican Students Association, the Lehman College Puerto Rican Students Association, the Bronx Community College Dominican Students Association, the Progressive Dominican Community Association (i.e., Asociación Comunal de Dominicanos Progresistas), Moria Bookstore (i.e., Librería Moria), and the Dominican Educators Council (i.e., Consejo de Educadores Dominicanos) (Stevens-Acevedo 1992d).

Also, at some point during his tenure, Linares' Dominican identity and his commitment toward the Dominican community were questioned, as epitomized by his public statement "Dominicanness by example" (i.e., *Dominicanidad con el ejemplo*) in which he called the community to recognize the purity of his Dominicanness and vote for his reelection as councilmember (Stevens-Acevedo 1991). Meanwhile, his popularity city-wide was high, as his efforts to control violence and pacify the community, as well as his position against Donald Trump's plan for the treatment of solid residues were widely applauded and granted him a *New York Post* recognition as the best councilmember of the year in 1993 (from among the City's fifty-one councilmembers). He also received a recognition from *The Village Voice* newspaper as the best among the twenty-one new councilmembers in the city in 1992 (Stevens-Acevedo 1993d). And at a time when the HIV-AIDS pandemic was as its highest level, Linares received the support of the LGBTIQ+ community when he joined other mayor's office members in their decision not to participate in the Irish American Saint Patrick's Day Parade if the organizing committee tried to hinder the participation of gays and lesbians in the event (Arroyo 1992). In addition, a public school (P.S. 4) named after the Dominican Republic's national hero Gregorio Luperón was built in School District No. 6 in Washington Heights.[8]

During this period, the Dominican Parade and Festival played an important role in the visibility of electoral candidates and the local engagement of the Dominican community. The Parade was a political tool that called the attention of local institutions to the needs and demands of the Dominican community. And because Dominicans had limited spaces in which to maneuver their political interests, the Parade's organizing committee was a competitive zone where leadership confrontations took place (Chacón 1990; Guillén 1990b).

This period was also characterized by a surging conservative wave that pushed for anti-immigrant policies nationwide, epitomized by the passage in 1986 of the Immigration Reform and Control Act (IRCA) that made it illegal to knowingly hire undocumented immigrants, and California's Proposition 187, also known as the "Save Our State" (SOS) initiative, passed in 1994 to establish a state-run citizenship screening system and ban undocumented immigrants from using non-emergency health care, public education, and other services in California. In addition, in 1995, New York Governor George Pataki signed legislation reinstating the death penalty (which had been previously abolished in 1984), and it went into effect until it was declared unconstitutional in 2004.

Dominican activists, such as university student leader Ydanis Rodríguez from the Dominican Youth Union (i.e., Unión de Jóvenes Dominicanos), saw those measures as an expression of the "conservative war against ethnic minorities," particularly Hispanics, addressed at hindering educational opportunities for undocumented children and the children of undocumented immigrants, as well as criminalizing ethnic and racial Hispanic and African American minorities through the construction of jails in the city (Hernández 1995a). The growing Dominican American community, represented by several grassroots organizations, such as the Mamá Tingó Women's Organization (i.e., Organización de Mujeres Mamá Tingó), the Youth Committee Against Budgetary Cuts (i.e., Comité de Jóvenes contra los Recortes), and the Dominican Youth Union, joined National Health Care Workers Union 1199 in street protests against these government's measures. In addition, Councilmember Linares, Democratic leader Espaillat, and the Dominican Alliance's (i.e., Alianza Dominicana) President Rafael Lantigua joined Puerto Rican and African American elected officials in their campaign against these conservative policies—that also included budgetary cuts due to the economic deficit provoked by U.S. Presidents Ronald Reagan's and George H. W. Bush's international warfare policies that affected the health care programs in the city (Hernández 1995b).

Throughout the 1990s, Dominican Americans nurtured an active political participation in the United States while maintaining close links with the Dominican Republic. Their electoral participation in U.S. politics grew steadily, particularly following the 1994 constitutional reform in the Dominican Republic that provided émigrés with the right to hold dual nationalities. The constitutional reform increased the participation of Dominicans in U.S. politics as it prompted many emigrants to naturalize and acquire U.S. citizenship and cast votes in local, state, and federal elections while remaining involved in the politics of the Dominican Republic (Graham 1996). In an interview with Linares, he stated that the participation of Dominican Americans in U.S. electoral politics was linked to the future of the Dominican Republic and that dual citizenship would help strengthen the presence of Dominican Americans in the United States and the U.S. naturalization process. Linares stated:

> As long as we could become an economic force in the United States, we will be able to influence the politics of this country toward our own.
>
> (Campo 1996b)

In addition, the active involvement of Dominican American leaders in the politics of the Dominican Republic was exemplified by the frequent news reports about Linares' statements on issues regarding the Dominican Republic. Nonetheless, in the early stages of the approval of the dual citizenship law, some social activists in New York City criticized the links of Dominican American leaders to political parties on the island as a hindrance to their active participation in U.S. politics, as it detached local leaders from the needs of their communities and delayed their prospects for political empowerment in U.S. elections (Stevens-Acevedo 1995). In addition, following the approval of the dual nationality constitutional modification, some Dominican American community leaders such as attorney Víctor Espinal criticized the fact that politicians from the Dominican Republic visited New York with the sole goal of seeking campaign funds despite the ongoing mistreatment that Dominican Americans received at the hands of the Dominican government and Dominican consular officials (Domínguez 1999).

The growing political empowerment of Dominican Americans in the United States was complemented by their involvement in the Dominican Republic's electoral contests, as some of their local community leaders, who were also the diaspora's overseas representatives of the major Dominican Republic's parties, believed that Dominicans in the United States expected to return one day to their homeland.

For example, when Rafael Lantigua, President of the Dominican Alliance and of the Dominican Revolutionary Party (i.e., Partido Revolucionario Dominicano) in New York, was asked about how he could explain the vibrant electoral mobilization of Dominican Americans for the 1996 elections in the Dominican Republic even though most of them could not vote, he said:

> We envision to return to a better motherland. We are economic exiles; we are not here because we like the cold weather but because the living conditions in the Dominican Republic did not allow us to stay there. It is currently said that two thirds of those residing in the island want to leave and this is very sad.
>
> (Campo 1996a)

Silvio Torres-Saillant, Director of the CUNY Dominican Studies Institute, linked the Dominican Americans' enthusiastic participation in the Dominican Republic's electoral politics to several factors, including their dream to return to their homeland, the economic and social benefits that it purported to those who supported the winning candidate, and the sincere vote of mostly humble people who trusted their favorite candidate. In a newspaper interview, Torres-Saillant stated:

> Among those who massively participate in the Dominican Republic's politics there are the ones who still keep alive the hope to return, but also there are others who expect being benefitted by the political changes thanks to the favors of the person that they support. There is the one who sees it as a possible area of investment to get, for example, a consulate [position] if his candidate wins. And let's not even talk about what this means in terms of the prosperity that he could achieve with that post. New York is a mine. Supporting a candidate is also a means to gain social importance. And there are those who donate their twenty dollars when politicians come with their saddlebags. That people feel genuinely committed to a candidate whom they trust.
>
> (Campo 1996a)

The media of this period contrasted the vital importance of the diaspora financing electoral politics in the Dominican Republic (particularly by Dominican immigrants in New York) with the apathy of the Dominican Republic's population toward its political leadership, as they did not expect any socioeconomic change coming from their politicians and instead preferred to rely on the remittances sent from their relatives for their subsistence, particularly from those relatives living in the United States (Campo 1995).

Conclusion

As it has been analyzed in this chapter, the Dominican American community has been actively engaged in the U.S. politics, particularly since the 1980s and 1990s. But, although it was a highly mobilized community, it gained little access to local electoral positions due to the lack of U.S. citizenship status of most of its members, a pattern that has been common among other Latino/a/x communities (as examined in Chapter 3). Notwithstanding, the previous political experience of some of its members in their homeland allowed them to build up political capital in the United States by taking advantage of pluralistic institutional spaces, such as Area Policy Boards (APBs) and Community School Boards (CSBs), and redistricting policies, organizing naturalization campaigns, and starting to build an electoral leadership that matured and rose up politically in the subsequent decades (a process described in the forthcoming chapters).

Therefore, as the Dominican case attests, on one hand, theories that sustain the importance of previous political participation in sender countries as an essential tool for immigrant social mobilizations and electoral participation in the recipient nation are applicable in this case (Leighley and Nagler 2016). On the other hand, theories that argue that the lack of citizenship status restricts immigrants' political empowerment to strict participation at the grass-roots level are not (Potochnick and Stegmaier 2020).

In this context, the Dominican case represents a paradigm in the study of political participation and representation by Latino/a/x immigrant communities in the United States. Dominicans hail from a fervently mobilized society, at least since the assassination of dictator Rafael Leonidas Trujillo in 1961 (an episode of national liberation that was nevertheless followed by the cruel murder of the plotters and their families), when rampant social mobilizations and a short-lived democratic attempt with the election of Juan Bosch in 1962 allowed Dominicans to taste the sweet flavor of democracy after a thirty-year-long bloody dictatorship. This experience, in turn, led many to fight for Bosch's reinstalment when a coup d'état overthrew his legitimate government, followed by a civil war and U.S. military occupation in 1965 and the imposition of Joaquín Balaguer's autocratic regime in 1966. Many Dominican youths who went into exile to the United States from the 1940s through the 1970s, and those who migrated in the 1980s and 1990s seeking better socioeconomic opportunities, praised the pluralistic political climate reigning in the United States and saw it as the perfect opportunity to start building up a political enclave in New York City that gradually branched out to other cities and states, despite all the barriers faced by them as a result of their immigrant, racial, and ethnic statuses, and the language barrier.

Notes

1 Interview with Anthony Stevens-Acevedo, September 24, 2023, via telephone and WhatsApp message app.
2 Interview with Anthony Stevens-Acevedo, May 17, 2023, via Zoom.
3 Interview with Anthony Stevens-Acevedo, May 17, 2023, via Zoom.
4 Interview with Anthony Stevens-Acevedo, May 17, 2023, via Zoom. Interview with Anthony Stevens-Aceveno, September 24, 2023, via telephone.

5 Interview with Anthony Stevens-Acevedo, May 17, 2023, via Zoom.
6 Interview with Anthony Stevens-Acevedo, May 17, 2023, via Zoom.
7 This was also a difficult time for the city of Los Angeles, where a major outbreak of violence, looting, and arson took place on April 2, 1992, in response to the acquittal of four White policemen connected with the severe beating of an African American man the previous year. See Wallenfeldt 2022.
8 In a 1992 news release, community activist and educator Anthony Stevens-Acevedo proposed the name of Gregorio Luperón for the new school in Washington Heights. See Stevens-Acevedo 1992f.

2 The Consolidation of Dominican American Political Empowerment in the 2000s

Alliances and Conflicts

The first two decades of the twenty-first century mark the takeoff of Dominican Americans as a significant political minority in the United States. This chapter analyzes the importance of community organizations in accelerating their political engagement through initiatives addressed at increasing voter turnout, such as the ones implemented by the Dominican American National Roundtable and Dominicanos USA. In addition, this chapter reflects on the long-standing political career of Ydanis Rodríguez and the role played by veteran Dominican American leader Adriano Espaillat in increasing the community's electoral representation through his political strategies and projects, as well as his endorsement of emerging leaders. It also discusses Espaillat's conflict with former acolyte Marisol Alcántara. Finally, it examines the undercount of Dominican Americans in the 2000 U.S. Census, as well as how their demographic characteristics and socioeconomic development help understand their strengths and weaknesses at the electoral level.

The Growth of the Dominican American Population and Its Electoral Participation

At the turn of the twenty-first century, the participation of Dominican Americans as voters in the U.S. elections was at the core of the political debate among the community's leadership. Veteran and youth leaders joined Cid Wilson in the Dominican American National Roundtable (DANR) and in 2002 launched an initiative to increase Dominican American voter registration and turnout at the congressional district level as a strategy to involve them into the fabric of the U.S. politics.

DOI: 10.4324/9781003497455-3

These leaders expected that their assessment would serve as a tool for grassroots organizations and the community at large:

to take the appropriate steps to increase the level of services and program funding dedicated to educate, orient, and facilitate political participation and civic awareness among Dominicans at a congressional district level, primarily through the study of the number of Dominican U.S. citizens of voting age.

(Dominican American National Roundtable 2004)

Meanwhile, the large concentration of Dominican Americans in New York City started to gradually diminish due to an outward migration that was subsequently reinforced by direct immigration from the Dominican Republic to newer Dominican American enclaves elsewhere throughout the United States. The Dominican American population of New York City declined from 73.4% of all Dominican Americans in 1980 to 65.1% in 1990 and to 53.2% in 2000 (Hernández and Rivera-Batiz 2003, 4). By 2000, there were Dominican Americans residing in each one of the United States' 435 congressional districts. In addition, the top 100 congressional districts with more than 500 registered Dominican Americans included states as diverse as Alaska, Delaware, Florida, Georgia, Illinois, Maryland, Michigan, New Hampshire, New Jersey, New York, and Virginia— as well as the District of Columbia[1] (Dominican American National Roundtable 2004).

The DANR report and other academic studies indicated that the Dominican American population in the United States was improperly counted by the U.S. 2000 Census. Approximately 1,041,910 Dominican Americans resided in the United States as of 2000, but the U.S. Census Bureau accounted for just 799,768 individuals of Dominican origin. Hernández and Rivera-Batiz (2003, 14) came up with this adjusted population figure based on the number of persons who completed U.S. Census questionnaires and explained the undercount as a result of the U.S. Census Bureau's failure to identify and properly count significant portions of the minority populations residing in large metropolitan areas (see Table 2.1).

By the early 2000s, 99% of Dominican Americans were concentrated in urban centers, with 53.2% of them in New York City. Dominican Americans held the highest U.S. naturalization rate at 57%, compared to other new Latino/a/x immigrant groups such

Table 2.1 Dominican-origin Population in the United States, 2000

Official U.S. Census count	799,768
Revised estimate	1,041,910
Difference	242,142

Source: Hernández and Rivera-Batiz 2003, 14.

as Salvadorans (43%) and Colombians (54%), although the overall percentage of Dominicans with U.S. citizenship status was lower when compared to Cubans (73%) and Mexicans (63%). In addition, 80% of Dominican American youth under the age of eighteen (who represented one-third of the entire Dominican American population in the United States) held U.S. citizenship. Based on domestic population projections prepared by the U.S. Census Bureau, a report estimated that the residential Dominican American population would increase from 3% of the entire U.S. population in 2000 to nearly 10% by 2020 and, if registered, 50% of adult Dominican Americans would be eligible to vote in U.S. elections (Dominican American National Roundtable 2004).

The DANR report highlighted the dichotomy between the increasing number of Dominican American individuals becoming involved in the U.S. political process and the community's lack of voter registration and mobilization, which in turn translated in it being underserved in terms of monies allotted to Dominican American neighborhoods to meet their housing and infrastructure, health care, and education needs. The report further stated that by the early 2000s, the New York City public school system had the lowest graduation rate in the country, with Dominican Americans representing the second largest Latino/a/x group in the system with 10.4% of all students. In addition, 31% of Dominican Americans in New York City did not have any health insurance coverage, compared to 18% of Puerto Ricans, 21% of Cubans, 35% of Mexicans, and 33% of other Latino/a/x ethnic groups (Dominican American National Roundtable 2004).

In 2013, Dominicanos USA (DUSA) was established to focus on the civic, social, and economic integration of Dominican Americans and the U.S. naturalization process with the goal of increasing their participation in U.S. elections. DUSA's efforts came at a time when Dominican American leaders were running for political office in New York and Rhode Island, as well as trying to take on a prominent political role all around the United States (Sosar 2018). When DUSA asked people of Dominican descent why they wanted to become U.S. citizens, some of them responded: because they wanted to vote (De La Hoz 2021). Dominican Americans were significantly inclined to vote as Democrats to support their platform of social justice issues, including immigration reform, health care, criminal justice, and economic improvements (Sosar 2018).

DUSA was founded as a nonprofit organization with offices in the Bronx, New York City, and sponsored by the Vicini family, the wealthiest oligarchs in the Dominican Republic and one of the largest owners of the country's sugar industry. The Vicini family invested approximately $3.5 million dollars in DUSA from 2014 through 2016 to canvas neighborhoods populated by Dominican Americans in New York City (particularly District 15th in the South Bronx that represented the largest Dominican American population in the city), Providence, and Rhode Island. DUSA's work was addressed at registering any Dominican American person who was eligible to vote in order to amplify the Dominican Americans' collective electoral clout. DUSA's leaders believed that Dominican Americans had still to fulfill their civic and political potential to influence U.S. politics and policy decisions. Through the use of algorithms provided by data companies such as Catalyst and Amicus, DUSA identified the districts where Dominican Americans were expected to reside in, and they sought out individuals at their home addresses (The Bronx Free Press 2014).

In a report, DUSA states that the organization registered, educated, and mobilized over 150,000 Dominican voters from 2013 to 2015 (DUSA 2017). It asserts that its voter registration and political mobilization efforts helped Dominicans reach a higher political recognition following the election of Adriano Espaillat as the first Dominican-born U.S. Congress Representative in 2016, and the nomination of Tom Perez, the son of Dominican immigrants, as the chairperson of the Democratic National Committee in 2017. DUSA affirms that political campaigns, however, have historically neglected the Dominican American community and, therefore, the latter has not received the necessary engagement, voter outreach, and information addressed at increasing its electoral participation.

In a DUSA telephone survey conducted among 800 registered and non-registered Dominican Americans from New York and Rodhe Island, participants were asked why they were not registered to vote: 38% responded that they did not know, 25% said that they did not receive enough information about the candidates, 20% indicated that they did not know how to register, 9% expressed that they believed voting doesn't make a difference, and 8% responded that politicians don't care about them (DUSA 2017, 5). The lack of information contrasted with their concern for social issues related to immigration, education, housing, health care, and discrimination against the Latino/a/x population. Almost all of the respondents expressed having strong preferences for the Democratic Party as the only one that cares about Hispanics. In addition, Dominican American registered and non-registered voters identified as a transnational community interested on issues concerning both the United States and the Dominican Republic and showed a strong desire to see more Dominican American elected officials and serving community groups to reflect their growing numbers: 79% of registered voters said that they would be more likely to vote if they had a chance to elect the first ever Dominican American to Congress and 78% of non-registered voters indicated that they would be more likely to become registered if given an opportunity to see a Dominican elected to Congress, and 74% of registered voters and 87% of non-registered voters expressed that they would be more likely to vote or to register to elect more Dominican Americans to the city council or office of mayor. In addition, 71% of registered voters and 79% of non-registered voters expressed their concern about the need of more local Dominican-focused civic advocacy groups that helped raise the voice of Dominican Americans (Latino Decisions 2015).

The need for electoral information was critical to increase the participation of a fast-growing population that in 2015 included approximately 1,914,120 inhabitants in the United States, representing 23.3% of the Hispanic population in New York, 33.5% in Rhode Island, 18.7% in Massachusetts, 15.2% in New Jersey, 11.5% in Pennsylvania, 7.5% in Connecticut, 3.6% in Maryland, 2.4% in Georgia, 2.4% in North Carolina, and 2.1% in Virginia (U.S. Census Bureau 2016; DUSA 2017, 9). In addition, seven out of every ten Dominican Americans were U.S. citizens in 2016, including 45% U.S.-born and 55% foreign-born, which made of Dominican Americans a significant share of Latino/a/x eligible voters in the country, particularly in the East Coast.

As shown in Table 2.2, the largest percentage of eligible Dominican American voters (from the overall Latino/a/x electorate) was concentrated in Rhode Island, followed by New York, Massachusetts,

Table 2.2 Dominican American Share of Latino/a/x Eligible Voters in U.S. Eastern States, 2014

State	Number of Latino/a/x eligible voters	Number of Dominican American eligible voters	Dominican American share of Latino/a/x eligible voters (%)
Connecticut	280,000	11,511	5.1
Florida	2,557,000	135,521	5.3
Georgia	291,000	9,603	3.3
Maryland	199,000	9,950	5.0
Massachusetts	372,000	61,380	16.5
New Jersey	831,000	116,792	14.0
New York	1,882,000	394,897	20.8
North Carolina	248,000	8,432	3.4
Pennsylvania	400,000	33,693	7.5
Rhode Island	68,000	20,196	29.7
Virginia	277,000	5,817	2.1

Source: DUSA 2017, 12.

New Jersey, Pennsylvania, Florida, Connecticut, Maryland, North Carolina, Georgia, and Virginia. (DUSA 2017, 12–13, 16).

Increasing the electoral participation of all ethnic minorities was also debated at the municipal level for the New York City 2001 municipal elections, when term limits forced thirty-six of the fifty-one City Council members into retirement, and in which over 175 second-generation Latinos/as/xs, Asian, and West Indians were running for City Council positions. This happened at a moment in which an estimated 55%–60% of New Yorkers were either foreign-born or the second-generation children of immigrants, according to the City's Planning Department figures (Casimir 2000). The 2000 U.S. Census revealed that—for the first time in history—Latino/a/x individuals outnumbered African Americans in New York City, and one out of every five voters in the city's electorate was foreign-born, with ethnic voters making up two-thirds of those voting for the first time in New York City (Jordan 2001). The "sleeping giant" that Dominican Americans, other Latinos/as/xs, and various ethnic voters represented, had been historically neglected by the political establishment of the Democratic Party because they looked different from their traditional constituents. Therefore, many aspiring ethnic politicians saw the Democratic Party as a hindrance to their electoral aspirations (Sachs 2001).

Table 2.3 Dominican-origin Population in the United States and New York
City, 1980–2000

Year	U.S. Dominican-origin population	New York City Dominican-origin population	New York City Dominican-origin population as a percentage of U.S. Dominican-origin population
1980	170,817	125,380	73.4%
1990	511,297	332,713	65.1%
2000	1,041,910	554,638	53.2%

Source: Hernández and Rivera-Batiz 2003, 20.

The significant demographic growth of Dominican Americans (as
shown in Table 2.3) had important effects in the councilmanic race
for District 10th, which encompassed the Dominican enclave of
Washington Heights and Inwood in New York City, as Dominican
Americans were becoming pivotal players in New York City politics.

Demographic Profile and Socioeconomic Development of Dominican Americans from 2000 to 2022

During the first two decades of the twenty-first century, the Dominican
American population in the United States continued to grow, with
an average annual rate growth of 4.8% from 2000 to 2010, and an
average annual growth rate of 4.4% from 2010 to 2020 (see Table 2.4).

The driving forces behind the Dominican American population
growth were immigration from the Dominican Republic and a surging
Dominican American population born in the United States, particularly
from 2010 to 2020. That steady demographic growth made Dominican
Americans the fifth largest Latino/a/x group in the United States, after
Mexicans, Puerto Ricans, Salvadorans, and Cubans. The largest concentration of Dominican Americans still resided in New York State as
of 2020 (particularly in the Bronx, New York City), but there was a
significant spread of Dominican Americans into other states, such as
New Jersey, Florida, Massachusetts, Pennsylvania, Rhode Island, and
Connecticut (Hernández, Rivera-Batiz, and Sisay 2022a, 4–5).

The current socioeconomic status of Dominican Americans still
reflects comparatively low incomes and subsequent relatively high

Table 2.4 Dominican-origin Population in the United States, 2000–2020

2000	1,041,910 (revised estimate)
2010	1,537,558
2020	2,216,258

Source: Hernández, Rivera-Batiz, and Sisay 2022a, 4.

poverty rates, particularly when compared with the overall U.S. population, but it also suggests increasing income rates and reduced poverty levels throughout the years. Dominican American annual average household per capita income was $22,551, which represents just 61% of the per capita U.S. average household income of $36,990. Also, 19% of Dominican Americans lived in households with incomes under the poverty line in 2019, compared to the overall U.S. poverty rate of 12.4% and the Latino/a/x poverty rate of 17.3%. However, the Dominican American community experienced one of the highest average rates of growth of per capita household income of any major racial and ethnic group in over twenty years, with incomes (as a percentage of average per capita household income in the United States) rising from 50% in 1999 to 57% in 2009 and to 61% in 2019. This positive trend, in turn, reduced Dominican American poverty rates from 27.5% in 1999 to 25.6% in 2009 and just 19% in 2019 (Hernández, Rivera-Batiz, and Sisay 2022a, ii).

Demographic data indicates that the high poverty rates among Dominican Americans from 2000 to 2020 are due in part to the age structure of the population, as they tend to be younger on average than the rest of the U.S. population (just like in the 1990s) and, therefore, this makes for a significant difference in terms of income. The overall Dominican American population in the United States had a median age of about thirty-two years in 2020 (almost like the overall median age of the U.S. Latino/a/x population which was thirty-one years) that is substantially lower than the median age in the United States (which is forty-three years). The highest levels of poverty among Dominican Americans are found in the elderly and children. Among older Dominican Americans (those over sixty-four years of age), about one-third (32.6%) lived in households that were poor, which is more than triple the poverty rate for the overall U.S. elderly population (at 9.5%) and substantially higher than the poverty level among the elderly Latino/a/x population (at 17.5%). Child poverty among Dominican Americans is recurrent in households headed by separated, divorced, or single women, as their income is lower than that of married couples. For example, while 13% of Latino/a/x children living in households with married couples were poor, the poverty rate for Latino/a/x children in female-headed households was 41%. In addition, the low socioeconomic status of Dominican Americans is due to the high proportion of recent immigrants within its population, who tend to have a lower income because their adjustment to the U.S. labor market takes time. Dominican immigrants who moved to the United States from 2010 to 2020 had average annual earnings of $25,622, while those who had immigrated to the country in the earlier period from 2000 to 2009 had higher wages, equal to $38,354 on average (Hernández, Rivera-Batiz, and Sisay 2022a, iii–iv).

The participation of Dominican American women and men in the U.S. labor force has increased, particularly when comparing it with their labor participation rate during the 1990s, which helps explain their growing per capita incomes and reduced poverty rates during the first two decades of the twenty-first century. The proportion of Dominican men participating in the labor force is significantly above that of the overall U.S. male population: 74.4% compared to 68.6%, respectively. Among Dominican American women, 64.7% were participating in the labor market (as of 2020), compared to 58.8% among the overall U.S. female population (Hernández, Rivera-Batiz, and Sisay 2022a, iv–v).

However, the unemployment rate for the Dominican American population was higher than the overall U.S. population in 2019. It was 6.5%, compared to 4.5.% for the overall U.S. population, and 5.1% for the U.S. Latino/a/x population; while in New York City, it was higher, 8.6% compared to 5.3% for the overall population of the city, and 6.6% for New York City's Latinos/as/xs in general. This data correlates with the higher unemployment rates in New York State and New York City (where Dominican Americans concentrate), which were 8.6% and 7.6%, respectively. Age has a major influence on the unemployment rate as joblessness is more prevalent among the very young (16–19 years of age): a rate of 24.5% for the entire nation, and even higher in New York City, with a 38% youth unemployment rate. The impact of the COVID-19 pandemic was devastating on both the Dominican American and the overall U.S. population, negatively impacting per capita incomes and poverty rates in 2020 (Hernández, Rivera-Batiz, and Sisay 2022a, v, viii).

The sectorial distribution of Dominican American workers in the United States is similar to the overall U.S. population. They are clustered in the service sector (44.9%) and the wholesale and retail sector (23.2%), which are also the top industries for the overall U.S. labor force (40.2% and 20.7%, respectively). Dominican Americans also feature prominently in the transport, communications, and public utilities sector (with 10.2%). They are, however, very underrepresented in public administration (2.4% compared to 4.5% for the overall U.S. population) (Hernández, Rivera-Batiz, and Sisay 2022a, vi).

The educational attainment of Dominican Americans is lower than for the overall U.S. population but is relatively higher than for the U.S. Latino/a/x population in general. By 2019, 22.6% of Dominican Americans twenty-five years of age or older had not completed a high school education, compared to 9.6% in the overall U.S. population, and just 19.6% had completed a college degree compared to 33.2% in the overall U.S. population. The proportion of Dominican Americans who had some college education was 20.7%. Among U.S. Latinos/as/xs, the proportion of those who had completed a college degree was also 19.6%, but the proportion of those who had some college education was 17.6%. In addition, U.S.-born Dominican Americans have a greater educational attainment than foreign-born Dominican Americans. Also, the college enrollment rates of Dominican American youth exceed those of the overall U.S. and Latino/a/x populations (Hernández, Rivera-Batiz, and Sisay 2022a, vii, viii).

The Coming of Age of Dominican American Electoral Representation

The first two decades of the twenty-first century also saw an increasing representation of Dominican Americans in U.S. electoral politics, as the community started to consolidate its domestic political identity and machinery on the path toward electoral power. Socioeconomic issues such as educational reforms that prioritized dual language acquisition and robust early childhood education, as well as support for small businesses, and the protection and expansion of affordable housing, were the main issues included in the agenda of Dominican American electoral candidates, as they had been long valued by the community. Health care also took on a prominent place in community debates, with the spread of the COVID-19 pandemic and its deadly effects among Dominican Americans, due to long-standing health disparities and the faulty response of local and state leaders (De La Hoz 2021).

A new generation of Dominican American politicians recognized the importance of the civic engagement that began three decades ago among the early Dominican immigrant community in New York City as a catalyst to its political empowerment. New York City Councilwoman from District 34th Diana Reyna (who served from 2001 to 2013) stated that: "The civic organization work began before the electoral victory [and built up] the structural organizations that were necessary for a community to survive in despair" (De La Hoz 2021).

There were seven Dominican American candidates seeking the seat left vacant by Guillermo Linares in the City Council in 2001, and all of them emphasized the importance of immigrant rights, education, housing, social services, and ending police abuse in their working-class community. The candidates included: Víctor Morrisette-Romero (director of the Association of Progressive Dominicans), who was supported by Linares; Miguel Martínez (director of the Washington Heights and Harlem Child Care/Domestic Violence Network), who was backed by Adriano Espaillat; Ydanis Rodríguez (CUNY student activist and public school teacher at the Gregorio Luperón High School), who received the support of the powerful Hospital Workers Union 1199 and local leader Dr. Rafael Lantigua; Roberto Lizardo (president of the Community School Board 6 and a supervisor with the city's Health Department); Giovanni Puello (special assistant at the Manhattan Borough President's Office); Ruben Darío Vargas; and Santiago Pina.

Miguel Martínez won the election to the City Council in 2001, and Lizardo and Rodríguez came in second and third place, respectively. Then, Lizardo and Rodríguez challenged Martínez again in 2004, but Martínez won the seat for another term. Martínez's opponents accused him of receiving campaign contributions from dozens of landlords with violations on their buildings, a particular sensitive issue for a community in which most residents are tenants. This issue had been previously raised in the late 1990s by Espaillat's opponents Evangelista and Morrisette during his campaign for the New York State Assembly race (Jordan 2001; Hicks 2003).

Table 2.5 shows that for the 2004 U.S. congressional and municipal elections, twenty Dominican American officials were elected throughout the U.S. Northeast, in the states of Maryland, Massachusetts, New Hampshire, New Jersey, New York, Pennsylvania, and Rhode

Table 2.5 Dominican American Elected Officials in the United States, 2004

Name & Party Affiliation	Position	City/County & State
Ercides Aguasvivas (Democrat)	Councilman	West New York, New Jersey
Marcos Devers (Democrat)	Councilman	Lawrence, Massachusetts
Adriano Espaillat (Democrat)	State Assemblyman	New York, New York
Juan Gómez (Republican)	Councilman	Worcester, Massachusetts
Carlos González (Republican)	State Representative	Manchester, New Hampshire
Julio Gurdy (Democrat)	Councilman	Allentown, Pennsylvania
William Lantigua (Independent)	State Representative	Lawrence, Massachusetts
Luis León Tejada (Democrat)	State Representative	Providence, Rhode Island
Miguel Luna (Democrat)	Councilman	Providence, Rhode Island
Miguel Martínez (Democrat)	Councilman	New York, New York
Carlos Matos (Democrat)	Councilman	Lawrence, Massachusetts
Joseline Peña-Melnyk (Democrat)	Councilwoman	College Park, Maryland
José Peralta (Democrat)	State Assemblyman	Queens, New York
Tomás Pérez (Democrat)	Councilman	Montgomery County, Maryland
Juan Pichardo (Democrat)	State Senator	Providence, Rhode Island
Diana Reyna (Democrat)	Councilwoman	Brooklyn, New York
Tilo Rivas (Democrat)	Councilman	Union City, New Jersey
Ramón Rosario (Democrat)	Councilman	Atlantic City, New Jersey
Manuel Segura (Democrat)	Councilman	Trenton, New Jersey
Vivian Viloria Fisher (Democrat)	County Legislator	Suffolk County, Long Island, New York

Source: Dominican American National Roundtable 2004, 63.

Island. The elected candidates included two councilwomen and eleven councilmen, one county legislator, three state representatives, two state assemblymen, and one state senator. State senator Juan Pichardo from Rhode Island held the highest office for a Dominican American elected official in the United States.

At the community level, the turn of the century marks the emergence of "Dominicans 2000," an organization integrated by young Dominican Americans, most of them university students and professionals, such as Raquel Batista, Lilliam Pérez, Julissa Reynoso,[2] and Marisol Alcántara (among others) that advocated for the creation of a national political agenda for Dominican Americans in the United States with the participation of leaders from the diaspora and the Dominican Republic. They launched an international conference with First Lady Hilary Clinton as the keynote speaker, which attracted approximately one thousand attendees who participated through coalitions with the Latino/a/x and Black communities. Raquel Batista, long-term community activist, attorney at law, former New York City Council candidate, and one of the leaders of Dominicans 2000 stated that,

> Many people were seeking the support of this group because it was formed by professionals, voters, and U.S. citizens. There were people who participated who were also advancing their own agenda in the Dominican community. For example, Ydanis Rodríguez ran for New York City Council after Dominicans 2000, and we supported him.[3]

Members of the Dominican Republic's Dominican Workers' Party (i.e., Partido de los Trabajadores Dominicanos, or PTD) supported the creation of Dominicans 2000. The PTD was active in New York City and was looking for the establishment of a political agenda in the United States. Among their leaders was Radhamés Rodríguez (a.k.a. Radhamés Pérez), a political exile who was in prison during the authoritarian regime of Joaquín Balaguer, as well as Juan Villar and Ydanis Rodríguez (among others). As pointed out by Batista,

> They helped to articulate the mission of the movement and supported us by developing the political ideology. They also supported our own professional work and participated in the marches and rallies organized by the Northern Manhattan Coalition for Immigrant Rights (NMCIR), of which I was the executive director.[4]

In addition, Dominicans 2000 received the support of Dominican American intellectuals, such as Silvio Torres-Saillant and Junot Díaz, politicians like the Dominican American Adriano Espaillat and the African American Virginia Fields, as well as community leaders such as Moisés Pérez, Rosita Romero, and Rafael Lantigua. In addition, members of Dominicans 2000 supported the agenda of U.S. politicians, including the New York State Senator Eric Schneiderman. Besides the conference, Dominicans 2000 launched a pre-college tutoring program to instruct high school students on the appropriate use of the English language for their college applications.[5]

From 2013 to 2014, several Dominican American officials were forced to resign from their elective posts after getting involved in illicit actions. Among them, were: former Democratic New York City Councilman Miguel Martínez, who pleaded guilty to charges of fraud and money laundering (Rivera and Barbaro 2009); former Democratic State Assemblywoman Gabriela Rosa, who pleaded guilty to charges of making false statements to immigration authorities and providing fraudulent data in bankruptcy court (Odato 2014); and former Democratic State Assemblyman Nelson Castro, besieged by accusations of living a double life and lying to investigators (Kochman 2014). Martínez resigned from the New York City Council in 2009, when federal prosecutors who were investigating a nonprofit group into which he directed city funds prepared to file criminal charges against him (Rivera and Barbaro 2009). After Martínez's resignation, Ydanis Rodríguez occupied the Democrat City Councilmanic seat from District 10th.

Ydanis Rodríguez and His Long Tenure as New York City Councilman

Ydanis Rodríguez was elected to the New York City Council in 2009, with the support of Citizen's Union and the endorsement of Assemblymember Adriano Espaillat and the Working Families Party. During his campaign, Rodríguez promised to carry out an administrative reform that would bring back integrity to the district. He affirmed that he would work to increase educational opportunities by changing the selection method for parent coordinators so that they were not hired directly by school principals. He also promised that he would provide school programs for children under five years old and vocational schools to deliver training to the community and small business owners. In addition, he vowed to increase the community's involvement in the city budget process, protect the rights of tenants, and improve public health and accessibility to farmers' markets (Citizens Union 2009). Rodríguez, who was reelected in 2013 and 2017, occupied his seat for a total of eleven years, during which he received a top recognition from the Human Rights Project in 2014 for sponsoring 187 bills from

2010 to 2013 that focused on housing, worker's rights, criminal and juvenile justice, health, disability rights, government accountability, and voting rights (Pereira 2014). In 2020, Rodríguez introduced a bill to allow non-U.S. citizen residents of New York City to vote in local elections. Through the campaign entitled "Our City, Our Vote," a citywide coalition of forty-five policy and immigrant rights organizations joined Rodríguez and other members of the New York City Council in support of the bill addressed at expanding the right to vote in municipal elections for New York City residents who were legal U.S. permanent residents or had a work permit. This campaign was launched at a time when nearly one million New York City residents could not vote in local elections due to their non-U.S. citizenship status, despite their tax contributions and investments in the development of the city (Maisel 2020).

During his long tenure as councilmember, Rodríguez brought about changes in transportation, education, economic development, housing, police reform, health care, and environmental policy. He is also the co-founder with Alexandra Soriano-Taveras, Johanny García, Julissa Reynoso, and Hypatia Zoquier, of the Pre-University Program of Dominicans 2000, addressed at providing educational, professional, and leadership support to recently arrived immigrant youths (Union Square Awards, 2002).

Following the completion of his tenure at the New York City Council in 2021, Rodríguez was nominated by Mayor Eric Adams as Commissioner of the Department of Transportation, a position that Rodríguez received in exchange for his strong support of Adams' electoral campaign. During his first year in the post, Rodríguez passed sixteen bills to improve safety for pedestrians and cyclists (Harlem World 2022).

The Preeminence of Adriano Espaillat in U.S. Politics

By 2020, the Dominican American community had achieved a fairly significant political representation, mostly by young leaders, some of them backed by the prominent Dominican American politician and Democratic U.S. Representative for New York's 13th Congressional District Adriano Espaillat, who stated in an interview: "I think that there is a great crop of young leaders that are emerging now, and

I think they want to take it to another level. And I'm really happy to see that" (De La Hoz 2021).

Currently known as the preeminent political broker north of Central Park in New York City and the leading Dominican American elected official in the United States, Adriano Espaillat has built what is known in the local political argot as the "Squadriano" (Coltin 2022): named for his powerful machinery based on a multipronged political partnership and assertive strategies to successfully back Dominican American candidates to elective posts. This electoral machinery has been made possible due to Espaillat's long-standing experience in the U.S. electoral arena since the early 1990s, during which he has occupied several positions as New York district leader, state assemblyman, and U.S. congressmember.

Adriano Espaillat's multidirectional strategy includes a meticulous work ethic addressed at getting the job done by working together with his lieutenants in the same campaign events, fundraisers, and elections, and hiring the same people to work on his campaigns term after term. In addition, he brings to his campaigns hundreds of political volunteers associated with his political club, Northern Manhattan Democrats for Change, who get the neighbors out to vote and hang flyers addressed to constituents at subway stops and polling sites. This grassroots strategy allows him and his political protégés to beat rivals who rely on large donors and labor union endorsements.

Some political observers, stunned by Espaillat's wins, particularly at neuralgic moments when Democratic county organizations have lost power, have employed different terms to describe his political style. Some say that he is a "political animal" with "a turnout machine rarely seen in New York City politics." Others consider him "a politician who approaches politics with a long-range perspective and thinks about the future," and "someone who is willing to take chances" (Cruz 2021; Coltin 2022). After the August 2022 Democratic primaries, Espaillat asserted:

> We've been here, we've been as a club. Northern Manhattan Democrats for Change was started back in 1993 when I was elected district leader. And it's still going strong. We tried to empower a community that at one point felt that it did not have a voice. And I think we've done a tremendous job in doing that.
>
> (Coltin 2022)

Several of Espaillat's opponents in the Latino/a/x community, however, call him a "pseudo-county leader" who is "obnoxiously diligent" and seeks to increase the political representation of Dominican Americans for the sole purpose of building his own political power. But Coltin (2022) has stated:

> The decisions Espaillat make will last long after he is retired or gone. It's not power for power's sake, these elected officials are in office, holding hearings, passing laws and most importantly providing constituent services to their districts with big Dominican populations.

Also, in his evaluation of Espaillat's guidance to his disciples, Shaun Abreu has attested: "We pride ourselves on being the future generation of leaders, which Adriano has done very well in terms of cultivating. He wants us to use the power that we have for the betterment of our community" (Coltin 2022).

In a fifteen-month period from 2021 to 2022, Espaillat successfully backed six candidates, including: Carmen De La Rosa, who originally served as Espaillat's campaign manager and was elected as New York State Assembly member from District 10 in Northern Manhattan (Washington Heights, Inwood, and Marble Hill) in 2016 and as City Councilwoman in 2021; Pierina Sánchez, who was elected as City Councilwoman from District 14 in the Bronx; Oswald Feliz, who won a City Council seat from District 15 in the central Bronx in 2021; Shaun Abreu, elected as New York City Councilman from Manhattan's District 7 in 2022; Manny De Los Santos, who was also Espaillat's campaign manager and won a seat in the New York State Assembly from District 72 in Upper Manhattan and the Bronx in 2022; and George Álvarez, who was elected as New York State Assemblyman from District 78 in the Bronx.

Espaillat's record during the 2019–2020 legislative session defines him as among the most progressive U.S. Congressional members. His record shows that he introduced or co-sponsored forty-three bills and resolutions that cover the following issues: health care, Caribbean Basin security partnership initiative to prioritize disaster resilience, housing survivors of major disasters, victims' compensation funds, excessive force prevention and accountability act, small business recovery grants, transportation alternative enhancement, green climate fund authorization, no federal funding for confederate symbols, support for early college high schools and concurrent enrollment programs, federal death penalty abolition, e-waste export and recycling, family reunification, preserving overseas immigration services, transportation alternatives, pay off of rental arrearages of low- and moderate-income households during the public health emergency related to COVID-19, preserving federal housing assistance, tax benefits for empowerment zones, ensuring justice for Malcolm X and reopening the investigation into his assassination, reaffirming the United States relationship with the Dominican Republic, ghost guns, condemning racism in sports, recognizing the impact of climate change on vulnerable and disadvantaged communities, recognizing women's and Black history months, prohibiting the construction of new border barriers, supporting the goals and ideals of Juan Pablo Duarte Day,[6] recognizing the contributions of Dominican American cultural community leader Normandía Maldonado, supporting the goals and ideals of Dominican Heritage Month, and recognizing the Dominican community's presence and contributions to Hamilton Heights, Washington Heights, and Inwood (Govtrack).

However, Espaillat has been criticized for receiving campaign donations from corporate political action committees and conservative organizations, such as the American Israel Public Affairs Committee. In response, Espaillat stated that he is not rich and defines himself as "one of the poorest members of Congress," which makes it difficult for him to ask his poor constituents (including *bodega* owners) to make campaign donations of a thousand dollars each (Coltin 2022). At a time when progressive political representation appeals to reject corporate donors, Espaillat's campaign style is seen as fairly conservative.

Espaillat's support for former union organizer Marisol Alcántara for her election as New York State senator for District 31 (which Espaillat left to run for the U.S. Congress) has also been seen as a conservative move (Coltin 2022). Initially, Espaillat consistently backed Alcántara, even though it became clear that she would join the Independent Democratic Conference (IDC) in Albany—a group of legislators that had a power-sharing agreement with Republicans. Although Alcántara did not publicly commit herself to the IDC during her campaign, on the night of her victory, her spokesperson announced that she would be joining its ranks in Albany (Sanchez 2018). Two years later, Espaillat pulled his support for Alcántara's reelection in 2018 and she and five other former IDC members lost to progressive challengers in the New York Democratic primaries.

Aquino (2021, 76) pointed out that Alcántara's alliance with the IDC was unfortunate given the timing of her decision. He asserted that the IDC, whose members are pejoratively known as "breakaway Democrats," was created in 2011 by former New York State Senator Jeff Klein. It operated without any major issues through the alignment of its members with the Republican Conference that denied Democrats control over the State Senate. But this pattern changed drastically following the election of Pres. Donald Trump in 2016 and the strong rejection in New York City of anything that could be associated with his controversial persona.

Espaillat's lack of support for Alcántara's reelection led to bitter gender-related tensions between the male political "connoisseur" and the female novel Dominican American politician. Espaillat said that he appraised some of Alcantara's achievements as New York State senator, including the allocation of funds to help immigrants that the New York State Senate and Governor Andrew Cuomo had created; but that he had also counselled her several times to leave the IDC because he believed it was hampering the legislative progress in the State Senate, so much that when the IDC got dissolved, he applauded that movement. Alcántara argued that as a woman she could do whatever she wanted and that Espaillat wanted to destroy and humiliate her by saying that her loyalty to Republicans was in response to their economic support to the tune of hundreds of thousands of dollars (Niedzwiadek 2016; Cruz Tejada 2018).

Indeed, Alcántara's campaign was sponsored by the IDC with a nearly $100,000 donation, and this support allowed her to grow in rank at a moment when she was being overlooked for support by most Democratic officials and clubs, labor unions, and others (Niedzwiadek 2016; Sánchez 2018). But the IDC was also criticized for helping to block the passage of key progressive legislation such as the Dream Act and the Reproductive Health Care Act, both key issues that Alcántara said that she supported in her reelection campaign. Alcántara refuted the idea that joining the IDC affected her decision-making in Albany by stating, "I have never taken a vote in the Senate that has been against my principles, as a trade unionist or as an immigrant, and as Latina. So, I'm very proud of my record" (Sánchez 2018).

Alcántara also asserted that several progressive bills such as marriage equality, raise the age for youth offenders, paid family leave, and free college tuition were passed through a Republican-IDC led State Senate. In addition, at the top of her agenda was the issue of immigration rights, including the Dream Act, as well as a bill that she co-sponsored to allow undocumented immigrants and their children access to state financial aid for college, and a farmworkers' rights bill. In addition, during her two-year tenure as state senator, she said she secured over $7 million in state funding for her district, using these funds to develop community-based organizations, such as Upper Manhattan's first LGBTIQ Youth Homeless Center, and the establishment of the Immigrant Defense Fund, which provides free legal services to documented and undocumented immigrants. Also, she invested $500,000 toward implementing a pilot program that works to reduce class sizes for English language learning students. In addition, she addressed issues related to Latina suicide rates and the deaths after childbirth of African American women and women of African descent (Sánchez 2018).

Marisol Alcántara's contingent alliance with the IDC follows a common practice among female politicians, in which they make alliances with diverse sectors, including conservative sectors, while looking for support for their progressive agendas. This strategy—which is also frequent among male politicians—is, however, highly criticized when employed by women, particularly in the U.S. male-dominated political world, where female politicians are often ignored by their own parties and presumed "natural allies." Reaching across the aisle constitutes, moreover, a common practice among female politicians in other countries; for example, in the Dominican Republic and other Latin American nations where female legislators from progressive groups contingently ally themselves with their conservative counterparts to guarantee the approval of key legislation that mainly benefits disadvantaged sectors (Jiménez Polanco 1999a, 2011).

Another salient attribute of Espaillat's successful leadership is his capacity to make unbounded alliances with politicians from diverse ethnic and racial backgrounds, as well as with former opponents, and with others who have run without his support. An example of the former is Espaillat's long-term alliance with Jewish American State Assemblymember Jeffrey Dinowitz and his son, New York City Councilman Eric Dinowitz, his close ties with African American New York State Senator Cordell Cleare and New York State Assemblymember Inez Dickens, as well as his alliance with Puerto Rican New York City Councilwoman Diana Ayala. An example of the second is Espaillat's alliance with Manhattan Borough President and former district leader Mark Levine, who ran against him in the 2010

Senate State primary for the seat left vacant by Eric Schneiderman (Campbell 2012). An example of the latter is Espaillat's alliance with New York State Assemblywoman Yudelka Tapia, who was not originally a part of his political clique and then became an insider. Espaillat's support for candidates outside the boundaries of his district is also noticeable, such as the case of Eric Adams during his run for New York City mayor, Tali Farhadian Weinstein during her candidacy for Manhattan District Attorney, and Francisco Moya in the New York City Council's speaker race of 2021 (Coltin 2022).

In addition, it is relevant to notice that Espaillat's growing political ambitions led him to unsuccessfully challenge the embedded power of African American U.S. Representative Charles Rangel, known as "the Lion of Harlem," in back-to-back elections in 2012 and 2014. Espaillat then went on to beat Rangel's ally, Assemblyman Keith Wright, following Rangel's retirement in 2016. Espaillat's triumph in New York's District 13 made him the first Dominican American member of the United States Congress and the first Latino to represent Harlem after seven decades of representation by an African American. The other Dominican American candidate in the race was Espaillat's long-term rival, Guillermo Linares, who was allied with Rangel and Wright (Paybarah and Skelding 2016; Neuman 2016).

By 2016, the Black population in District 13 had decreased to 27%, while Latinos/as/xs comprised 52% of residents, which exposed boiling tensions with racial overtones during the campaign. The tensions resulted from the redrawing of the district in 2012 that forced African Americans and Latinos/as/xs to compete for the same congressional seat. Espaillat stated that the unfair redrawing of the district (a practice known as "cracking"), which divided ethnic strongholds into several districts, disenfranchises minorities and would lead to "20 years of nuclear political war" (Paybarah 2012; Paybarah and Skelding 2016).

Espaillat's preeminent leadership has been sometimes marred by rumors about his alleged orchestration of the resignation of some of his opponents, amid investigations or criminal charges, as a means to eliminate his political opposition (Coltin 2022). However, these assertions remain as rumors with no facts to support those accusations.

The consolidation of Espaillat's political leadership comes at a moment when there is a generational change in the political representation of Latinos/as/xs in the United States. Espaillat is well aware of that shift, and his current political protégés hail from the Millennial and Xer generations, which reflects his compliance as a Baby Boomer with the progressive values of the younger generation that has come to represent the largest voting block among his constituents.

Espaillat, who defines himself as a moderate "progressive and practical" politician, has remained involved in New York City's local politics while serving as a representative to the U.S. Congress. He explains his involvement as a means to ensure "fairness, representation, and for communities to move forward together." In that context, Espaillat stated:

> I believe that more women should be in government. I believe that race matters. I believe that ethnicity is important. And that everybody should have a seat at the table. And that's, I think, the fundamental piece of being progressive. If you cannot wrestle with that and get it done, everything else is just window dressing. Harlem deserves to have Black leadership, East Harlem or El Barrio deserves to have Puerto Rican leadership. If you cannot understand that there's a million Dominicans in New York City and we deserve to have a seat at the table, what can be more progressive than that?
> (Coltin 2022)

As examined in this chapter, Dominican Americans have faced numerous challenges while coming of age in U.S. electoral politics in the early 2000s, including the disparity between the large number of candidates and a limited number of voters; a conundrum that drove several organizations such as the Dominican American National Roundtable and Dominicanos USA to focus on bolstering voter registration and mobilization. Since the mid-2000s, DUSA has continued to work on organizing the U.S. naturalization process of Dominicans and fueling an increase in their voting turnout.

A significant accomplishment is the growing number of Dominican Americans who have become elected officials at the federal, state, and municipal levels throughout the Union. A myriad of new, young candidates for elective office has been endorsed by veteran leaders, such as Guillermo Linares, Ydanis Rodríguez, and Adriano Espaillat, the longest serving elected officials in the history of the Dominican American community. Moreover, there are now political races free of rivalries between Dominican American leaders—different from what we saw in the 1980s and 1990s. The main difference is that whereas old conflicts aroused between Guillermo Linares and

Adriano Espaillat—the only two prominent Dominican American leaders during the late twentieth century—in the 2000s, political conflicts centered on Espaillat versus younger leaders, such as Marisol Alcántara. Espaillat, however, has maintained a solid grip on political power and has been easily reelected to Congress since 2016, the highest elective office that a Dominican American has ever won in the United States. This record, consequently, exposes him to criticism from his opponents both inside and outside the Dominican American community for his personal style and political strategies.

As a national leader, Congressman Adriano Espaillat has developed one of the most progressive congressional agendas, as it has been analyzed in this chapter. In addition, he maintains strong links with the Dominican American community through his organization "Dominicans on the Hill" that convenes an annual event to recognize the accomplishments of prominent Dominican figures and the contributions of the Dominican American community to the United States. It counts on the participation of top U.S. political, academic, cultural, and business figures. Moreover, Espaillat nurtures friendly relations with other minority groups, such as the Puerto Rican and the LGBTIQA+ communities through the annual Puerto Rican and Pride Breakfasts. Finally, Rep. Espaillat has played a significant role in U.S.-Dominican Republic relations by getting involved in critical bilateral issues, such as his defense of Dominican immigration policies and his advocacy for the removal of a U.S. travel alert for the Dominican Republic over accusations of racism (Bredderman 2017; Dominican Today 2023). His concerns for U.S.-Dominican Republic issues work in tune with the transnational identity of the Dominican American community.

Notes

1 The District of Columbia does not have a congressional representation, but its voters get three electors during U.S. presidential elections.
2 Julissa Reynoso was appointed as Ambassador of the United States to Uruguay during Pres. Barack Obama's administration and Ambassador of the United States to Spain during Pres. Joe Biden's administration.
3 Interview with Raquel Batista, October 9, 2023, via Zoom.
4 Interview with Raquel Batista, October 9, 2023, via Zoom.
5 Interview with Raquel Batista, October 9, 2023, via Zoom. Interview with Lilliam Pérez, September 28, 2023, via Zoom.

6 Juan Pablo Duarte was a Dominican writer, activist, poet, military leader, liberal politician, and one of the founding fathers of the Dominican Republic. As one of the most celebrated and racially inclusive figures in Dominican history, Duarte is considered a folk hero and a revolutionary visionary in the modern Dominican Republic as he recognized the ample spectrum of Dominican racial identity. Duarte was the son of an impoverished Spanish merchant who had seen his father's business ruined under Haitian domination. Along with mixed/Black leader Francisco del Rosario Sánchez and military officer Ramón Matías Mella, Duarte organized and promoted the secret society known as "La Trinitaria," a political movement that eventually led to a revolt against the authoritarian regime of Jean-Pierre Boyer who ruled the island until his replacement by Haitian President Charles Rivière-Hérard in April 1843. The declaration of independence of the Dominican Republic from Haiti took place on February 27, 1844. As stated by Moya Pons (1995, 143), news of the overthrow of Boyer reached Santo Domingo on March 24, 1843, and it was marked by an atmosphere of agitation, conspiracy, and expectation. The news served as a signal for Boyer's opponents to take to the streets shouting, "Long live independence and reform!"

3 Latinos/as/xs in U.S. Politics

A Learning Path for Dominican American Political Empowerment

In this chapter, I examine recent literature on the engagement of Latinos/as/xs in U.S. politics. One key feature of this literature review is that there are several interesting analyses about Mexican Americans, Puerto Ricans, and Cuban Americans, but there is no reference to Dominican Americans as part of the Latino/a/x community, even though they represent the fourth largest Latino/a/x immigrant community in the United States and a significant ethnic voting bloc in the country's electoral arena. I analyze the primordial characteristics of these larger Latino/a/x immigrant communities that are determinant to their political involvement in the United States and whether, in some specific cases, they could be compared with the experience of Dominican Americans, as based on my own academic research. As detailed here, some Latino/a/x political experiences constitute good examples to follow for Dominican American political empowerment while others have already been replicated by Dominican Americans. Finally, there are some characteristics of the Dominican American political culture that could serve as a role model for other Latino/a/x communities. For example, the capacity that Dominican Americans have developed to take advantage of pluralistic community participation, forged by local institutions such as those found in the Area Policy Boards of the 1980s and the Community School Boards of the 1990s to advance their political leadership (as examined in Chapter 1).

DOI: 10.4324/9781003497455-4

Lack of U.S. Citizenship Status among Latinos/as/xs and Increasing Grassroots Participation

As pointed out by Potochnick and Stegmaier (2020), the lack of U.S. citizenship status limits the political development of Latinos/as/ xs which, in turn, drive many of them to engage only in grassroots mobilization. In the case of Dominicans, community engagement has been, nevertheless, a means to gradually develop political leadership and achieve representation at the electoral level (as examined in Chapter 1). The lack of U.S. citizenship status drove many Dominican Americans in the 1980s and 1990s to engage in Area Policy Boards and Community School Boards that eventually served as a platform to develop political engagement at the electoral level, as some members of the APBs and CSBs found there a suitable space to nurture their leadership and become candidates for elective office. In addition, besides their active participation in street mobilizations, Dominican American grassroots organizations have also been consistently investing in steering the new immigrant population toward the naturalization process as part of campaigns to increase the size of their electorate. As such, Dominicans constitute one of the most actively involved immigrant communities when it comes to naturalization campaigns. Their persistent efforts addressed at increasing the number of Dominican American registered voters speak volumes about an immigrant community that has a long-standing political participatory experience back home and that, therefore, has been very politically active in the host nation, particularly since the 1980s and 1990s, following its first massive immigration wave in the mid-1960s.

Increasing Participation in the 2000s Despite Language Barriers and Structural Discrimination

Latinos/as/xs have also experienced cultural obstacles to engage in mainstream politics, including language barriers and structural discrimination. However, Latinos/as/xs started to rise as a significant electorate in the second decade of the twenty-first century with most of them voting as Democrats and with a higher participation rate among middle-class, educated voters. It has been observed that certain factors, such as high levels of political engagement in their countries of origin, have a positive effect in the growing incorporation of Latinos/as/xs into U.S. electoral politics (Potochnick and Stegmaier

2020). When contrasting Dominican Americans with other Latinos/as/xs, it is noticeable that the former also strengthened their political participation and electoral representation in the 2000s (as examined in Chapter 2). Lewis-Beck and Stegmair (2016) suggest that, when compared to other Americans, Latinos/as/xs as an immigrant population are affected by the same political climate as all Americans and, therefore, are able to assimilate into new political environments and have common experiences with other Americans, including developing attachments to parties and having opinions on political issues, evaluating the state of the economy, and assessing political candidates.

Despite the obstacles to electoral participation posed by their lack of U.S. citizenship status, Latinos/as/xs started to transform the U.S. electorate by becoming its largest racial or ethnic minority in the early twenty-first century. In 2015, Latinos/as/xs made up about 15% of the voting population (Potochnick and Stegmaier 2020). For the 2020 presidential election, that proportion went down, with Latinos/as/xs representing just 10.2% of all eligible voters (approximately 16.5 million), which still translated into an increase of nearly 30% from the 12.7 million votes cast in 2016. A determinant factor in the increase of Latino/a/x voting has been the strategies implemented to motivate potential voters to register. But despite the observed growth, the lack of U.S. citizenship has left Latino/a/x voting lagging behind that of Whites (70.9%), African Americans (62.6%), and Asians (59.7%) (CLACLS 2021).

The lack of U.S. citizenship status of nearly a third of Mexicans (who represent the largest Latino/a/x cohort), for example, has limited their political participation to civic engagement, such as attending protests, rallies, volunteering, and writing to political leaders. In the 1960s, Mexican Americans participated in the Civil Rights Movement, and in the 1990s, California's anti-immigrant policies reignited their civil mobilization. In the early 2000s, Mexican political participation mostly developed through civic engagement in the face of anti-immigrant policies because of California's Proposition 187. In 2006, punitive federal anti-immigrant legislation that targeted undocumented immigrants ignited the nationwide *Gran Marchas*. Recent research shows high levels of participation across the political spectrum (e.g., political campaigns, voting, and civic engagement) among third-generation Mexican Americans (U.S.-born Mexican Americans with U.S.-born parents), similar to that of third-generation Whites. On the other hand, members of the second generation (U.S.-born Mexican

Americans with foreign-born parents) vote the least and are the less active in political campaigns (Potochnik and Stegmaier 2020).

Mixed Straight-line and Segmented Pattern of Mexican American Political Engagement

Potochnik and Stegmaier (2020, 529) point out that Mexican political incorporation follows a mixed-straight and segmented pattern. On the one hand, they follow a *straight-line* pattern of assimilation in which the first generation (non-U.S. citizen immigrants) encounter significant barriers to political participation, such as learning the cultural norms for participation, developing confidence in the use of the English language for political persuasion, and identifying policy-making access points. As these barriers lessen over time and across generations, each successive immigrant generation achieves a higher political involvement similar to that of White middle-class Americans. On the other hand, they also follow a *segmented* pattern, where their political participation is shaped by the context of reception (e.g., discrimination, structural access, and economic opportunities) and the power and influence of co-ethnic groups.

The mixed straight-line and segmented pattern of political participation followed by Mexican Americans is also evidenced in the emerging political incorporation of Dominican Americans in the early 1980s and 1990s and their growing participation and representation in the 2000s. As analyzed in Chapter 1, the structural barriers imposed by the lack of U.S. citizenship on the first immigrant generation (Dominican immigrants with foreign-born parents) that frequently entered the U.S. with tourist visas and gradually adjusted their status to become permanent residents or U.S. citizens limited their political participation to civic mobilizations and engagement in Area Policy Boards and Community School Boards, where U.S. residence or U.S. citizenship were not required. In addition, the power and influence of co-ethnic groups, such as Puerto Ricans and African Americans, contributed to the Dominican Americans' growing levels of representation.

Influence of Demographics in the Political Participation of Latinos/as/xs

Leighley and Nagler (2016) analyze the influence of demographics in the political engagement of Latinos/as/xs in the U.S. South,

California, Florida, and Texas, including factors such as education, income, gender, and age. The data examining self-reported voting turnout and participation suggests that foreign-born Latinos/as/xs who become U.S. citizens report voting at about the same rate as Whites (84.3% for the former, compared to 85.5% for the latter), and U.S.-born Latinos/as/xs report voting at a slightly lower rate (78.9%). Regarding the impact of educational levels on voting patterns, Latino/a/x high school graduates and those who failed to graduate from high school vote less than college graduates. Turnout is higher for foreign-born naturalized Latinos/as/xs with some college education than for U.S.-born Latinos/as/xs, which indicates a lack of interest toward politics among those who have been born in the United States, unlike the higher political interest shown by Latino/a/x immigrants. The turnout for foreign-born naturalized Latinos/as/xs with less than high school and with a high school diploma is 42.8% and 30.6%, respectively, and for U.S.-born Latinos/as/xs, it is 39.8% and 44.3%, respectively. The voting turnout for foreign-born naturalized Latinos/as/xs and U.S.-born Latinos/as/xs who have some college education is 55.5% and 50.2%, respectively. Foreign-born naturalized Latinos/as/xs citizens and U.S.-born Latinos/as/xs who are college graduates vote at a rate of 56.3% and 47.3%, respectively (Leighley and Nagler 2016, 153).

In addition, Leighley and Nagler (2016, 153) found a positive relationship between income and voter turnout, although the poorest foreign-born naturalized Latinos/as/xs vote at a slightly higher rate than U.S-born Latinos/as/xs. However, at the middle-low and middle-high income brackets, U.S.-born Latinos/as/xs vote at a higher rate than foreign-born naturalized Latinos/as/xs. Finally, at the top income level, foreign-born naturalized Latinos/as/xs vote at a much higher rate than U.S.-born Latinos/as/xs. The data indicates that foreign-born naturalized Latinos/as/xs and U.S.-born Latinos/as/xs earning less than $20,000 per year vote at a rate of 44.4% and 40.6%, respectively. Those with an annual income ranging from $20,000 to $40,000 vote at a rate of 35.7% and 46.7%, respectively. The voting rate of those earning from $40,000 to $80,000 per year is 38.4% and 45.3%, respectively, and those with an annual income of more than $80,000 vote at a rate of 72.0% and 49.9%, respectively. This data has left it clear that well-to-do Latino/a/x immigrants denote more interest toward political involvement in the United States than U.S.-born Latinos/as/xs.

Data regarding gender shows a similar voting pattern for foreign-born naturalized Latinos and Latinas and a slightly higher vote rate for U.S.-born Latinos. For foreign-born naturalized Latinos and U.S.-born Latinos, the voting turnout is 43.2% and 46.5%, respectively, while for Latinas, it is 43.2% and 44.2%, respectively. Results by age indicate that the youngest and the oldest age cohorts among U.S.-born Latinos/as/xs report high levels of turnout, while middle-aged foreign-born naturalized Latinos/as/xs also report a higher voting rate. The data shows that foreign-born naturalized Latinos/as/xs and U.S.-born Latinos/as/xs aged 18–34 vote at rates of 35.8% and 47.8%, respectively; those aged 35–44 vote at rates of 34.3% and 39.6%, respectively; those aged 45–54 vote at rates of 50.0% and 36.4%, respectively; and those aged 55 and older vote at rates of 47.6% and 50.1%, respectively (Leighley and Nagler 2016, 153).

In the case of Dominican Americans, although their educational attainment is lower than that of the overall U.S. population, their level of education was higher than that for the overall Latino/a/x population during the second decade of the twenty-first century and resulted in reduced poverty levels from 2010 to 2020 (see Chapter 2).[1] Paralleling this process of enhanced educational levels and reduced poverty, Dominican Americans experienced a noticeable increase in voting turnout and political representation, which allowed them to become a significant electoral ethnic minority community in the U.S.

Effects of Pluralistic Participation in Sending Countries on the Political Participation of Latinos/as/xs in the United States

In their analysis of self-reported turnout rates of naturalized U.S. citizens by their level of political engagement in their countries of origin, Leighley and Nagler (2016, 159) suggest that Latinos/as/xs who voted in their countries of origin were more likely to vote in the United States once they became U.S. citizens. If they were active in political parties in their own countries and paid attention to elections, they are usually more interested in elections in the United States. This analysis works in tune with the growing engagement of Dominican Americans in U.S. politics, as they hail from a highly politicized homeland that has effected significant structural changes, such as the right to dual citizenship, following its approval by the Dominican Republic's Congress. This constitutional right has motivated many Dominicans to become U.S. citizens so to be able to participate in U.S. electoral politics. Also, starting in the 2000s, Dominican American community organizations have been implementing strategies to increase naturalization rates, as well as Dominican electoral participation and representation (as examined in Chapter 2).

Effects of Lack of U.S. Citizenship Status on Latino/a/x Electoral Participation

In their study of participation among Latinos/as/xs in Miami for the 2012 U.S. elections, Jones-Correa and McCann (2013) found that civic status orients immigrants toward particular participatory venues. Latino/a/x citizens are more involved in campaigns and non-electoral participation, such as signing petitions and making financial contributions. Among non-U.S. citizens, those who are documented participate in social movements and grassroots communal activities, and those who are undocumented tend to do more volunteer work.

In this context, Brown and Bean (2016) take into consideration the fact that many Latino/a/x immigrants in the United States come as unauthorized entrants to denote the importance of initial societal membership among immigrants in their political incorporation, including the work done by local organizations and institutions, such as those with implications for immigrant settlement or the acquisition of U.S. citizenship. These factors were thoroughly examined among Dominican Americans in Chapters 1 and 2 by highlighting the seminal role played by Area Policy Boards and Community School Boards in the incorporation of Dominican Americans in U.S. politics in the 1980s and 1990s and the naturalization and voting mobilization strategies pursued by the Dominican American National Roundtable (DANR) and Dominicanos USA (DUSA) in the 2000s.

Also, as pointed out by Brown and Bean (2016, 23), gradations of legalization and U.S. citizenship relate positively to general political knowledge and other kinds of integration. In addition, sociocultural distinctiveness is envisioned as not incompatible with other forms of integration, which allows immigrant groups to maintain ethnic values and behaviors that are distinct from those of the U.S. mainstream and from those of other ethnic immigrant groups. This trend is epitomized in the gradual emergence of Dominican American political candidates and elected officials during the first two decades of the twenty-first century (following a period of increased naturalization rates for Dominicans), as well as society-wide acceptance of their visible participation in the Dominican Day Parade and other cultural expressions.

Preferential Role of Democrats over Republicans among Latinos/as/xs Voters

Studies on Latino/a/x partisanship show that they are more likely to become Democrats than Republicans, and even nonpartisan Latinos/ as/xs may have clear latent preferences for the Democratic Party over the Republican Party. During the 2020 elections, 62% of registered Latinos/as/xs identified with the Democratic Party and 34% with the Republican Party (Noe-Bustamante, Budiman, and Lopez 2020). In the 2012 presidential elections, Barack Obama received 71% of the Latino/a/x vote, which represented an increase from 67% in 2008 and from just 53% in 2004 (Huddy, Mason, and Horwitz 2016; Sears, Danbold, and Zavala 2016).

Sears, Danbold, and Zavala 2016 (2016, 183–187) state that the increased rates of deportations during the Obama administration lessened support for the Democratic Party among Latinos/as/xs. Also, while most Latinos/as/xs are Democrats, there are some who vote for the Republicans. On the one hand, the political hostility displayed by Republicans toward minorities has driven Latinos/as/xs even more toward the Democrats and, on the other hand, there are some Latinos/ as/xs who are "natural Republicans," due to their widespread social conservatism and upwardly mobile aspirations.

Huddy, Mason, and Horwitz (2016, 206) attest that Latino/a/ x identity converges with Democratic identity, as every year from 1984 to 2012, Latinos/as/xs have been more likely to identify with the Democratic Party than with the Republican Party. But Republican politicians have also pushed Latinos/as/xs toward the Democratic Party. In recent years, Republicans have engaged in a number of racist, ethnocentric, and xenophobic actions that have alienated and offended Latinos/as/xs, including anti-immigrant legislation, a negative rhetorical portrayal of Latinos/as/xs, offensive political campaign ads, and an unwillingness to consider immigration reform legislation.

In addition, Smith (2017) states that Latinos/as/xs have experienced stigmatization and discrimination due to the belief by mostly White voters, politicians, and poll workers that undocumented immigrants seek to vote in local elections. This has fueled an "illegal" Latino/a/x voter threat myth where mostly White voters fear that undocumented

Latinos/as/xs threaten their group status, as analyzed in his case study of Port Chester, New York. The documented exclusion of Latino/a/x voters led to a lawsuit by the U.S. Department of Justice against the town in 2006 for hampering the ability of Latino/a/x voters to elect candidates of their choice.

This case study reflects the common threat perceived by members of the White dominant group when subordinate ethnic groups become their competitors. As a result, the majority group subsequently attempts to block the incorporation of ethnic minorities into mainstream society, which frequently detonates inter-ethnic and inter-racial conflicts. This trend was exemplified by the political clash between veteran Irish American politician John Brian Murtaugh and emerging Dominican American leader Adriano Espaillat in the 1990s, when the former rejected the incipient political empowerment of Dominican Americans through their representation in Community School Boards (as examined in Chapter 1).

The 2019 Chicago Council Survey found deep divisions between supporters of Democrats and Republicans over immigration. Republicans see immigration as a critical threat to the United States, believe that restricting immigration makes the country safer, and support using military troops to stop migrants from crossing into the United States. Democrats, on the other hand, do not consider immigration a critical threat and their views on policy actions substantially differ from those of Republicans. About 78% of self-described Republicans view immigration as a critical threat, compared to just 19% of self-identified Democrats. Some 78% of Republicans believe that restricting immigration makes the United States safer, compared to just 24% of Democrats, and 81% of Republicans support the use of military troops to prevent immigration at the U.S.-Mexico border, compared to just 23% of Democrats. In addition, Republicans are more likely than Democrats to consider draconian immigration policy measures as more effective, like conducting more arrests and deportations (82% for Republicans, compared to 29% for Democrats). Also, 40% of Republicans support the separation of children from their parents when the latter are accused of entering the United States illegally, compared to just 10% of Democrats. In terms of border security, 93% of Republicans approve of increasing border security, compared to 55% of Democrats. In addition, 83% of Republicans agree that imposing new fines on businesses that hire undocumented immigrants is an effective policy, compared to 54% of Democrats (Hammer and Kafura 2019, 1).

Huddy, Mason, and Horwitz (2016, 207–209) also argue that Latino/a/x partisanship rests on preferences for a political party's policy stances on social or economic issues, including the Democrats' liberal stance on issues such as abortion, affirmative action, school vouchers, health care, gun control, and tax cuts. They argue that this support for the Democrats does not appear to be a direct defense of their self-interest because less well-educated Latinos/as/xs are only somewhat more likely to be Democrats than their better educated counterparts are, thus no connection can be made between low incomes and Democratic identification.

When examining Latino/a/x partisanship by national origin, it is noticeable that the two largest groups, Mexican Americans and Puerto Ricans, identify as Democrats, whereas Cuban Americans identify as Republicans. The 2000 Latino Voter Survey indicates that roughly 67% of Mexican Americans and 64%–69% of Puerto Ricans are Democrats, while 66%–69% of Cuban Americans are Republicans (Huddy, Mason, and Horwitz 2016, 206). Their country of origin and political background play an important role in the political identity of Latinos/as/xs. Whereas Mexico and Puerto Rico have had fairly long-standing democratic experiences, Cuba's brief democratic experience in the early twentieth century was followed by a right-wing personalistic dictatorship (that of Fulgencio Batista) and then persistent leftist authoritarianism (that of the Cuban Revolution) throughout the twentieth and twenty-first centuries.

Like the larger Latino/a/x voter population, Dominican American voters mainly identify with the Democratic Party's liberal socioeconomic stances; therefore, most Dominican American candidates and elected officials represent the Democratic Party (as examined in Chapter 2). Dominican Americans come from a country with a past rooted in a long-standing tradition of military dictatorships (the latest one under Gen. Rafael Trujillo, in power from 1930 to 1961) and authoritarian regimes (incarnated by Joaquín Balaguer, from 1966 to 1978). However, their democratic experience has lasted decades and goes back to the international opposition by Dominican exiles to both autocratic regimes, and then from the democratic opening of 1978 to the present. Nowadays, most voters in the Dominican Republic identify with liberal democracy (Jiménez Polanco and Sagás 2023).

Partisan Preferences and the Importance of Spanish-Language Media

Sears, Danbold, and Zavala (2016, 201) state that Latinos/as/xs clearly express their partisan preferences, including those Latinos/as/xs classified as outside the party system and non-naturalized immigrants who cannot vote in the United States. They also suggest that Spanish-language news media is one potential facilitator of Latino/a/x connections with the U.S. party system, as it helps politicize immigrants by promoting political awareness and engagement. In addition, Garcia-Rios and Barreto (2016, 79, 91) point out that although English-language media prevails in terms of availability, the popularity of Spanish-language media has been increasing exponentially in recent years. And, while the English language opens an important door into American culture, particularly through English-language media, Spanish-language media reflect the immigrant experience, reinforce ties to the home country, and effect a significant increase in the level of interest in voting among Latinos/as/xs.

Like other Latino/a/x communities, Dominican Americans clearly express their partisan preferences that are largely concentrated in the Democratic Party. On the one hand, coming from a national political structure where candidates from minor parties have few opportunities to compete in the political arena, Dominicans in the United States prefer to vote for mainstream party candidates. On the other hand, their consistent support for democratic ideals since the early 1960s (after the murder of dictator Rafael L. Trujillo) has been embedded in Dominican American political participation and representation in the United States, where most Dominican Americans voters and candidates advocate for human and citizenship rights, including educational, housing, and health care improvements. These democratic ideals had been already embraced by Dominican political exiles during the thirty-one-year-long Trujillo dictatorship, which allowed them to develop an international opposition to the regime headed by the Dominican Revolutionary Party (i.e., Partido Revolucionario Dominicano, or PRD) founded in Havana, Cuba in 1939 (Jiménez Polanco 1999). Not surprisingly, the liberal PRD won the first democratic elections held in the post-dictatorship Dominican Republic in 1962, a traumatic experience for Dominicans nonetheless as the government led by Juan Bosch only lasted seven months before being overthrown by a military coup on September 25, 1963.

In addition, as in the case of other Latino/a/x communities, the Spanish-language media actively covers Dominican American political engagement, as documented by the numerous citations from Hispanic news outlets utilized in this book and dating to the early political empowerment of Dominicans in the 1980s–1990s. The Hispanic and Dominican media have historically paid close attention to the political activity of Dominican American politicians in the United States with a copious narrative that goes deeply into details concerning their electoral competition, the candidates' platforms, their challenges, and their confrontations with opponents both within and outside their ethnic group, as well as criticisms and their achievements.

In essence, this literature review on Latinos/as/xs in U.S. electoral politics reveals similarities between Mexican Americans, Cuban Americans, and Puerto Ricans that create a unique opportunity to compare them with Dominican Americans. It also helps us reflect on the latter's challenges and achievements, some of them precedent setting, such as their capacity to build electoral leadership out of grassroots participation in Area Policy Boards and Community School Boards at a time when many of them did not have U.S. citizenship status and were facing a considerable language barrier.

Note

1 It is important to notice that this measure of the educational level of Latinos/as/xs (including Dominicans) in the United States is limited by their knowledge of the English language and does not apply to their educational level in their homelands that, in many cases, is above-average relative to their compatriots. Likewise, many Latino/a/x professionals who migrate to the United States are forced to forego their careers and take on low-paying jobs due to the difficulties in adjusting to a new language.

4 The Dominican American Leadership in Their Own Words

Challenges and Accomplishments

This chapter analyzes the role played by veteran and new Dominican American political leaders through interviews in which they ponder the main challenges and accomplishments of Dominican political activism in the United States. The interviews were conducted via Zoom with U.S. Representative Adriano Espaillat, former NYC Councilmember and New York State Assemblymember Guillermo Linares, former NYC Councilmember Ydanis Rodríguez, New York City Councilmember and former New York State Assemblywoman Carmen de La Rosa, and Rhode Island State Senator Ana Quezada.

The interviewer asked the following questions: When and how did the representation of Dominican Americans in U.S. politics emerge? What were the main challenges? What was your role in that process? What are the main issues concerning the Dominican American leadership? What have been the main challenges for Dominican American political leaders in their struggle for scarce political positions? Which are the most important aspects of your personal experience, including challenges and accomplishments? What are the main factors contributing to the evolution of Dominican American leadership and your role in the development of the community's political empowerment? Which are the main generational changes and challenges in the political perspectives of Dominican American leaders? What is the nature of the relationship between Dominican American leaders and Dominican political leaders in the homeland? How did the approval of dual citizenship by the Dominican Congress contribute to increase the participation of Dominican Americans in U.S. elections? What role did you play in the political efforts toward the approval of the

DOI: 10.4324/9781003497455-5

Figure 4.1 Adriano Espaillat. Unveiling New York State and local plans to become a safe haven for abortion access. Credit: Christopher S. Kelly. Flickr.

Dominican Republic's dual citizenship clause? How did the relationship between the Dominican American community and the Democratic Party develop? What have been the main challenges for Dominican American leaders to gain the recognition of the Democratic Party and eventually occupy political positions within the party? What are the future prospects for Dominican American political empowerment in the United States? The questions were slightly modified for some interviews, and not all questions were asked in some cases. The answers have been edited for clarity and length.

Interview with U.S. Congressman Adriano Espaillat

Adriano Espaillat became the first Dominican American elected to the U.S. House of Representatives in 2016. He previously occupied a seat in the New York State Senate from January 1, 2011, to December 31, 2016, and in the New York State Assembly from January 1, 1997, to December 31, 2010.

I interviewed Espaillat on November 27, 2023, and asked the following questions:

1. JJP: When and how did the representation of Dominican Americans in U.S. politics emerge? Which were their main challenges? What was your role in that process?

AE: It began in the 1980s, with the election of members of our community to what was called the Area Policy Board, an entity that was put together by New York City to fight poverty, hunger, and inequality in many neighborhoods. The city allotted a budget for different programs, including youths, food pantries, and school-based programs, and people from each district got elected and they didn't need to be U.S. citizens to vote in those elections. People like Normandía Maldonado, Hilario Albert, and Minerva Cury got involved and a good number of them got elected. The program is still around, although with a different name and members are no longer elected, they are appointed.

Later on, the Community School Boards emerged, and they also allowed non-U.S. citizens to vote, including undocumented parents who had kids in the schools. Sixto Medina was the first one elected and then some others, including Guillermo Linares, Apolinar Trinidad, George Acosta (who later became a judge), Raysa Castillo, and Anthony Stevens-Acevedo. The elections were done through the proportional representation system and ranked choice voting. The Community School Board selected principals and had a process to decide the budget for the school district. That was the groundwork for an effort to build over seventeen new schools in the district in order to accommodate over 3,000 kids that were being bused to the Bronx and Harlem because there was not enough space in Washington Heights for them. Thousands of parents registered to vote, and at one point, Dominicans became the majority representation in Community School Boards. It was probably the biggest investment in school construction in the state, if not the nation, and we were able to achieve that as we got the majority of the members of the school boards elected.

I was elected president of the local 34th Precinct Community Council in 1985. At that time, the public safety issue was becoming prominent for our community as we saw the emergence of crack cocaine in the city, and that pushed the overcrowding of schools to a second place over public safety issues. We saw an average of over a hundred homicides a year, and in one year, we had 122 homicides. Due to the district's proximity to the George Washington Bridge and the I-95 interstate highway, Washington Heights became a distribution center for crack cocaine in the 1980s and 1990s for the Tri-State and Northeast region. Many of the drug gangs were Dominicans and the drug trade evolved into a very violent exchange with rivals. Also, there were corrupt police officers that were involved in the drug trade themselves in the 34th Precinct and some of them were arrested and fired. That was a real problem because the drugs were being sold from apartments where our people lived. The drug traffic drove up rent prices because drug dealers were able to pay exuberant amounts of money for rented apartments and the landlords began to hike up the rent for everybody else, which was a serious problem. We were able to push back on that slowly; thus, we were able to go from one hundred homicides in one year to zero and then just five or six.

I ran in 1989 for City Council and lost, and a new seat was created in 1991 after the census, and Linares got elected as New York City councilmember, and I got elected as New York State assemblymember in 1996.

2. *JJP:* What are the main issues concerning the Dominican American leadership?

AE: What we need now is political discipline to be able to come together and speak as one block to the governor, the mayor, and to the president of the United States, understanding that we are not going to agree on everything, but we got to be together in the important decisions that we make in education, housing, culture, and our legacy. I've been working hard to try to get consensus among the leadership, which is difficult to do but it is so important. It comes through a great deal of maturity and our leadership is relatively young right now; they are all under fifty except for me. With maturity comes some level of ability to get consensus and develop political discipline. We need to document our presence and let people know that Washington Heights is the center of a rich culture. We need to develop that and make it a national story just like Chinatown is for Chinese people, like Little Italy is for the Italian community, like El Barrio is for Puerto Ricans, and like Harlem is for Black people.

3. *JJP:*   What have been the main challenges for Dominican American political leaders in their struggle for scarce political positions?

AE: A lot of stuff happens through redistricting. Districts are created or prevented from being created through the redistricting process that happens every ten years with the census. I got elected to the New York State Assembly back in 1996 because after the 1990 census, the 72nd assembly district was created, and it was very favorable to Dominicans. Guillermo Linares got elected to the New City Council because it got expanded to fifty-two members, and that was favorable to Dominicans. Even my congressional district runs into the Bronx and many Latinos gave me the opportunity to get elected. That doesn't mean that everybody has to get elected in a district that is mostly composed by Dominicans; there are Dominican candidates that get elected in districts that do not have many Dominicans and they are elected because of their own personal qualities and history.

4. *JJP:*   Mention important aspects of your personal experience (challenges and accomplishments) as one of the most prominent Dominican American political leaders.

AE: There are a bunch of legislative bills that I've passed and moneys that I've directed into the community. I have three major projects going on right now, one of which already began, which is the extension of the 2nd Avenue subway that goes through East Harlem. It's a seven-billion-dollar project. Also, the Kingsbridge Armory Project in the Bronx, for which the city has allocated one hundred million dollars and the state an additional one hundred million. It could be an economic incentive for the Bronx and the city. In addition, we are trying to get a first-class performing arts center for Dominicans in Washington Heights.

I have passed bills at all levels as a state assemblymember, including out-of-state tuition that allows undocumented CUNY students to pay the same levels of tuition that U.S. citizens pay, scholarships for the survivors of the American Airlines Flight 587 tragedy, and several monuments, among others. I have a whole history of bills, but for me, the most important piece of what I do is that I am an organizer at heart, and I want to see young people carry the torch for another fifty years. So, for that end, I try to keep the door open for other people to come in.

5. *JJP:*   What are the main demands and needs of your constituents?

AE: At the federal level the main issue is immigration. When I was a state senator and assemblymember, it was housing, which continues to be an important issue for my constituents.

6. *JJP:*   What are the main factors contributing to the evolution of the Dominican American leadership and your role in the development of the community's political empowerment?

AE: I try to promote young people, and as a result we got six young officials elected to the City Council. I am also trying to do that at the state level, and I go across the country trying to help other members to get elected to congress. I did so during these past couple of months with Sabina Matos in Rhode Island, several years ago with Juana Matías in Massachusetts, and I will continue to promote the election of Dominican officials. Also, I hold a meeting every year called "Dominicans on the Hill," which is now into its sixth year, where hundreds of Dominicans come from other states to Washington and bring with them their ideas.

7. *JJP:*   What are the main generational changes and challenges in the political perspectives of old and new leaders?

AE: I think that new leaders need to understand the genesis of all that we have been talking about today and that somehow every Dominican is connected, either through relatives or friends, and they share their experiences with the motherland, which is Washington Heights. When you know that, and you know your history you are strong.

8. *JJP:*   What is the nature of the relationship between Dominican American leaders and Dominican political leaders in the Island?

   AE: I think that young leaders now don't have the kind of relationship that myself, Linares, and Ydanis have, because generationally they are not as connected to what happens in politics back home. But they should, because if you have to pay, for example, $1,300 for an airplane ticket to go back home to visit your family, and you have two kids plus husband and wife, that's a lot of money and you may not be able to go. Thus, that's an issue that needs to be addressed, and when they ask me what is the big thing that needs change in the Dominican Republic, I say the price for airline tickets that needs to come down, because thousands of people go back home. I am currently working with the president [of the Dominican Republic] to see how we can lower the prices for airline tickets.

9. *JJP:*   How has the approval of dual citizenship by the Dominican Congress contributed to increase the participation of Dominican Americans in U.S. elections? What role did you play in the political efforts toward the approval of the Dominican Republic's dual citizenship?

   AE: We played a pivotal role in making sure that it was approved by Congress over there and it did help. Although I would say that it was not as decisive as the anti-immigrant provisions that were adopted through the antiterrorist legislation passed under the Clinton administration. It stated that if you were engaged in an offense of moral turpitude, meaning that if, for example, you were caught urinating on the streets, which would normally result in a summons, now you would have faced deportation. That drove many people to become U.S. citizens quickly, because they didn't want to get deported—more so than the dual citizenship.

10. *JJP:*   What are the future prospects for the Dominican American political empowerment in the United States?

   AE: We have to get somebody become president of the United States. I think somebody in our community will become mayor of the City of New York.

Figure 4.2 Governor Andrew Cuomo (right) participates in New York State's Annual Thanksgiving Food Donation Drive with Senator Adriano Espaillat (left) and Assemblyman Guillermo Linares (center). Flickr, November 24, 2015.

Interview with Former New York City Councilmember and Former New York State Assemblyman Guillermo Linares

Guillermo Linares was the first Dominican American elected as New York City councilmember for District No. 10 (northern Manhattan) in 1991. His tenure as councilmember lasted from January 1, 1992, through December 31, 2001. Afterward, he occupied the appointed position of Commissioner for the New York City Mayor's Office of Immigrant Affairs from 2004 to 2009. He became an elected official again as New York State Assemblymember for District No. 72 and occupied this position from January 3, 2011 to December 31, 2012 and January 1, 2015, to January 31, 2016. Since 2017, he occupies the appointed position of Commissioner of the New York State Higher Education Services Corporation.[1]

During my interview with Commissioner Guillermo Linares on October 24, 2023, via Zoom, I asked him the following questions:

1. JJP: When and how did the representation of Dominican
Americans in U.S. politics emerge? What were their main
challenges? What was your role in that process?

GL: It emerged with a movement created in Northern
Manhattan of whose leadership I was a part of. The
movement emerged with a wave of Dominican families arriving to Washington Heights primarily in the late
1960s and 1970s, and that continued in the 1980s. I was
involved because I became a bilingual teacher in 1975
soon after graduating from college. There was a need to
help organize newly arrived families and integrate them
in the new settings, dealing with their immigration status,
teaching them English, preparing them for the General
Educational Development test (GED), and navigating
the new and challenging system by creating the nonprofit Association of Progressive Dominicans, organized
from 1978 to 1980. It was a volunteer effort that involved
graduated students from CUNY, including teachers and
engineers.

When I was a teacher, it became very clear to me that
there was a need to collaborate in bilingual education
across the city of New York, thus I got involved with bilingual education across the city. We created a movement that
comprised activists who were mostly parents with children in public schools and were fighting for the creation of
bilingual education for the newly arrived immigrants. That
parents' movement got me elected in 1983 as a member
of the Community School Board in District No. 6, which
is located north of 135th Street [in Manhattan]. By the
time I was elected, we had already brough the first Latina
superintendent to oversee the school district of Northern
Manhattan. That led to the creation of a movement that
involved all the schools within that district. The decen-
tralization law allowed immigrant parents with children
in the public school system to register in the Community
School Boards even if they were undocumented or were
non-U.S. citizens. This allowed the mobilization in
three months of 10,000 parents who were registered in
Washington Heights and Inwood to participate in the 1986
Community School Board election. They represented half

of the parents registered in the entire city of New York. We saw that there was a movement that was taking off as School District No. 6 became the most overcrowded in New York City. We had kids learning in hallways, in classrooms, in auditoriums, and in cafeterias. I, myself, had forty-two students registered in my 5th grade class, thirty-eight of them attending every day. Thus, that became the number one crisis in Northern Manhattan—which was denounced in the papers by parents. The solution from the City was to put the students on buses and send them to other places. The community reacted with the creation of a movement led primarily by the Association of Progressive Dominicans that demanded that brand new schools were built in Northern Manhattan. That movement was the foundation for my election to the Community School Board on three occasions and then to the New York City Council. I became the first Dominican-born elected to public office in the United States and this happened fifteen years after working as a volunteer in Northern Manhattan organizing newly arrived immigrant families. As the 1989 Community School Board election approached, we said that we wanted to capitalize on that historical juncture and we learned that Mayor Edward Koch was running for a fourth term, and that he needed Latino support. We were on the media on a weekly basis blasting everybody to demand the construction of schools, thus Mayor Koch came up to Washington Heights and was received by 300 parents when he came to visit the schools, and there, because he wanted the support of Latinos, he publicly committed to build nine brand new schools in Northern Manhattan to address overcrowding (that was equivalent of over $500 million dollars). I attribute that victory to the parents' movement and the community organizing. That monumental accomplishment took place at a moment when we didn't have any elected officials, and that was the preamble for the community to ask me to consider leaving my position as a principal to become an elected official in the City Council.

2. *JJP:*   What are the main issues concerning the Dominican American leadership?

GL: By the time that I got elected in 1991 and assumed office in 1992, the community's attention had shifted from addressing overcrowding in schools to becoming the epicenter of drug distribution in the Northeast. Washington Heights was plagued by drug dealing and it was the distribution site for New York State's surrounding areas, including Upstate, New Jersey, Pennsylvania, Connecticut, Massachusetts, etc., and there were killings in the streets mainly by rival drug gangs. There was only the 34th Police Precinct in the Northern Manhattan community north of 155th Street, and in 1990 alone, there were 119 deaths in the streets of Washington Heights and the drug dealers were in charge, not the police.

Thus, the first thing I was asked to do as a newly elected official was to advocate for the community to get a brand-new police precinct. I went to see David Dinkins, the first Black mayor, and the police commissioner said that in three months they will give me an answer. But three weeks later, José (Kiko) García was killed by an officer. The community was disconnected from White police officers (who were outsiders) and there were terrible relations between the community and the police. The community took to the streets and there were riots. This happened a few weeks before the National Democratic Convention in the City of New York and just right after the Los Angeles riots and the Crown Heights mobilization.

Therefore, seeing Washington Heights burning up was my first challenge, and the focus of the entire city, the press, and the media was on me, asking what I could do about this as the newly elected Dominican. I stepped up and helped mobilize the community and also challenged the authorities, including the mayor, the police commissioner, and I said that we wanted a police precinct with trained, diverse officers to serve the community and a youth center that was designated later as Alianza Dominicana.

I organized twenty-two meetings and got the commitment for the new 33rd Police Precinct in three weeks. As a result, the homicide rate in Northern Manhattan lowered to only seven people in 1998.

3. *JJP:*   What have been the main challenges for Dominican American political leaders in their struggle for scarce political positions?

   GL: In 1992, when I was elected councilman, Bill Clinton was the presidential candidate in the Democratic Party, and he found out that besides Puerto Ricans having elected officials, there was a first Dominican elected in the United States. The bottom line is that I supported Bill Clinton only because he learned that there was a first Dominican elected official in the United States. I was introduced to him during the Democratic Party Convention.

At that moment, I realized that in the movement that I helped create with others in Northern Manhattan, the vast majority of Dominicans were not yet citizens. When I got elected, there was a handful of Dominicans that could vote. I had 1,500 volunteers in my campaign in 1991, and among them, there were new voters who were Jewish, Puerto Ricans, Cubans, Greeks, and African Americans, and there was a movement in which we were working in different fronts with other ethnic communities that had common challenges because they were our neighbors. Thus, it became clear to me that we needed to get involved in helping Dominicans to become citizens of the United States and also legal residents. Thus, we started a movement, and I brought the non-profit arm of the National Association of Elected Officials (NALEO) to Washington Heights to focus on naturalizing Dominicans. In five years, we were able to naturalize 5,000 new citizens in Northern Manhattan, and five years later, we were able to elect the second Dominican to the State Assembly.

The challenge that I learned is that one individual does not make change, but if that individual is connected to a movement, to an agenda. and a number of issues and challenges that the community feels strongly about (first it was overcrowding in schools, then it was public safety), that individual can gain access to political positions. Unless you have that, you cannot understand what would happen to the children and the newly arrived immigrant families that were working in factories or opening small businesses, and that what they just wanted was what my parents wanted: to have their kids go to high school and being able to have a voice and go to college and improve their lives to the next level. And that was what the movement we helped create was looking for, not forgetting where we came from but making sure that we were respected and recognized, and that our history will be acknowledged.

The bottom line is that unless you have a sense of identity, coalition building, and partnership with other communities that share the struggles that your community faces, it is very challenging to make inroads. In my case, I was one out of nine [Latinos] in the New York City Council, eight were Puerto Ricans, and I was Dominican, but I was the voice for immigrants as the first Latino immigrant in that position, and Latino immigrants gravitated toward me as they saw me already defending immigrants and public education, something that I had been doing for fifteen years.

One of the first things that I was able to do regarding the importance of highlighting history and culture was going to see CUNY Chancellor Ann Reynolds to negotiate the creation of the Dominican Studies Institute (DSI) because I felt that it was important that our history be told and shared with other ethnicities. The DSI was created in 1992. My last accomplishment as a councilmember was going to see Vice-Chancellor Jay Hershenson to negotiate the establishment of the Center for Latin American, Caribbean and Latino Studies (CLACLS) at the CUNY Graduate Center.

4. *JJP:*   Mention important aspects of your personal experience (challenges and accomplishments) as a Dominican American political leader.

  GL: Something that has stayed with me to this point where I find myself is that when I was leaving the Dominican Republic at the age of fourteen, I was the oldest of seven children. That meant that most of the time I was looking after my brothers and sisters. My mom was a seamstress in the small town of Cabrera. I spent half of my time with my grandfather who had a parcel of land of about eighty-eight acres (approximately 500 *tareas*) across the river. Thus, Papá Pedrito (Don Pedro Linares) taught me how to plant *yuca* (cassava), *yautía* (malanga), *plátanos* (plantains), *guandules* (pigeon peas), and everything that you could plant in a *conuco* (parcel of land). I learned the process of how *tabaco* was made then and that served me to become someone close to the land for the survival of the family—and that has never left me.

Eighth grade was the last year of schooling in my hometown and my mom realized that they could only send me to another big town to go to high school, so she convinced my father to move to New York. She worked in the garment industry in New York City, and three months later, she sent money, and my father came to New York in 1963. They overstayed their visas, they were undocumented, and in 1965, they got their green cards, they petitioned the seven of us and we came in 1966. I came with a 7th grade education not knowing a word of English. The most challenging time for me ever was having to compete with other students in high school without knowing English, only with my good behavior.

When I graduated with a general diploma, my counselor said that not everybody was suited for college, and I believed him. I felt so insecure that my father and my mother said, "oh, so you are thinking that you're not going to college? You are going back to the farm." My grandfather had passed away already. So, I said "oh, oh, I better go to college." And that's how I landed in City College, where I became active with the Dominican Students Association. I got elected as the president of the association. That year, we fought with the President of City College to establish the first Dominican Studies course, focusing on highlighting the contributions of Dominicans, as part of the Puerto Rican Studies Department.

In terms of my leadership, I am shaped by what I learned in college about the Dominican people and the Haitian people. But when we look at the leadership, it has been tailored by the interests of the United States. I saw this as part of the minority that emerged during the Civil Rights Movement, claiming the rights that they have, and that is a driving force for me everywhere I go and in every position that I take.

5. JJP: What were the main demands and needs of your constituents during your former positions as New York City councilmember and New York State assemblyman?

Bearing in mind that I was elected by a handful of my own nationals, the biggest challenge that I needed to overcome was to demonstrate to the other ethnicities that helped me get elected, and that would be at the table during decision making, that I could earn their trust and respect, that I could deliver for them given the needs and the challenges that they were facing. That was a true test for me because if I failed them, then the door could close, and the next Dominican would find it very difficult to get elected. One of the goals of leadership is looking for alliances and I did that as I realized that some of the needs that we had in my district were also the needs of the Bronx, Brooklyn, and even Staten Island. So, I looked to coalesce to make sure that resources that came to my community were also benefiting others. For example, based on my own experience with teachers, parents, and libraries, I went to see the Speaker of the New York City Council and proposed to initiate a pilot program that connected teachers in the classrooms with the local library and parents with children. The initiative was so successful in Washington Heights and Inwood that it was funded for the entire City. It was powerful because the only place for parents to go and get access to technology, internet, and books and not getting asked about their citizenship status was the library. That's how you bring partnerships to help children, families, and create a foundation for the community.

When I landed in the New York State Assembly representing Washington Heights, my first bill was the original New York State Dream Act, because I was very concerned that undocumented students graduating from high school did not have the opportunity to apply for financial aid. So, during my first two years in the Assembly (in 2011 and 2012), I mobilized all the advocates and partners that I could get to support the Dream Act, that included all the networks of immigrant organizations in the City and the State of New York, as well as the labor movement, the business community, and the education field. In 2017,

I got appointed to the position that I have in the agency in charge of providing financial aid. In 2019, finally, the Dream Act got approved and it landed on me.

6. *JJP:*   What are the main needs of New Yorkers during your current position as New York Commissioner of New York State Higher Education Services Corporation?

GL: I am the one in charge of rolling out the implementation of the Dream Act. Three years later after its approval, thousands of young students are receiving financial aid and have access to all twenty-seven programs that we have. I work closely with the New York State university system, the city university system, the Commission of Independent Colleges and Universities, and the Association of Private Colleges. Over 330,000 students receive financial assistance through my agency, and we distribute over $800 million dollars every year to students. I have always been an activist and right now I am looking to reform the agency. We are now focusing on a modernization effort that will take three years and is looking to reform, under the leadership of Governor Kathy Hochul, the TAP (New York State Tuition Assistance Program) to cover more students and serve students and families.

7. *JJP:*   Which are the main factors contributing to the evolution of the Dominican American leadership and your role in the development of the community's political empowerment?

GL: I believe that there's nothing greater than understanding and embracing the true issues affecting families in their communities, and the obstacles they face in making sure that their children have access to education and job opportunities, and to acknowledge and respect them for who they are and their background. Whoever does not have a sense of that will find it very difficult to lead communities and much less to help build a movement around the aspirations of that community. I live through that.

Some of us get elected to positions and they are temporary assignments that are given to us in our journey. If you lose sight that you are being given an opportunity to help facilitate and enhance the collective aspirations of people that you represent, you are lost. Also, we are mostly representing diverse communities that have arrived relatively recently, and we are present here, but our minds and hearts are also connected to our home country, the family that is there and dreams that we hope to pick up later. This means that we are here and also there, and it means being sensitive regarding what happens back home. The dynamic of our kids today, most of whom are second- or third-generation U.S.-born Dominicans, is different from the one we had in the 1970s, when most of them were new immigrants. The setting and the technology have presented many challenges. Thus, dual citizenship allows our children and grandchildren become citizens of the Dominican Republic while they are citizens of the United States. Dual citizenship builds stronger ties to our home country, history, and culture. I've been holding a torch, but the people that I work with in the movement they're all holding torches. Those torches were being held by others who made sacrifices before we came, they were Puerto Ricans and immigrants that came from other places, and they struggled to make things a little better for those who had been arriving in the 1960s and 1970s and even the 1990s. We have been holding that torch and we have to recognize that there is a commitment by us to hand that torch over to our children and those children who were able to enter college or specialize to make things better. We are raising the flag of humanity. Every struggle and challenge that we overcome is making humanity better.

8. *JJP:*   How did the approval of dual citizenship by the Dominican Congress contribute to increase the participation of Dominican Americans in the U.S. elections? What role did you play in the political efforts toward the approval of the Dominican Republic's dual citizenship?

GL: My biggest role has been helping Dominicans to become naturalized citizens of the United States from the very beginning in the 1970s and it is still ongoing, because that's what makes them dual citizens. Every time the country has needed my help I've been there, such as when the United States was crafting CAFTA, and the Dominican Republic was left out and Pres. Hipólito Mejía called me and asked to help get the Dominican be part of the trade agreement. I had a great relationship with Congressman Charles Rangel, and he had just become the chair of the House Ways and Means Committee, the U.S. Congress' most powerful committee, I went to see him and the next thing you see is DR-CAFTA (Dominican Republic-Central America Free Trade Agreement), and it put the Dominican Republic in the map. Thus, every opportunity I have in a leadership role I try to help the Dominican Republic.

While in the past we helped Dominicans to become citizens of the United States, now we are looking to help our children and grandchildren who were born in the United States to become citizens of the Dominican Republic. That brings a lot of potential for the young people in the Dominican Republic and in the United States to be able to devise strategies and a roadmap that will help them rescue the Dominican Republic and help elevate our potential in the diaspora.

9. *JJP:*   What is the nature of the relationship between Dominican American leaders and Dominican political leaders in the Island?

GL: I had been noticing for a very long time that whenever there were elections in the Dominican Republic, the candidates came to visit the diaspora to fundraise and make promises. They had also established chapters of their parties here to help further participation in those elections. Later, they allowed the diaspora to elect representatives to the Dominican Republic's Congress. But I have always seen that, in some ways, as an afterthought. I have never seen the leadership of those who have been elected go beyond the rhetoric to really tap the immense human capital that has been developed within the diaspora to facilitate the exchange of ideas, resources, and expertise in order to help the Dominican Republic.

I have been disappointed, but I've never lost hope for the young people, that's why I am so happy to be where I am now, helping kids and parents to acknowledge how powerful it is to get a college degree or to get specialized training so that at least they can get into the workforce and help their families. If we lose sight of our own Dominican history, we are lost, and that needs to be transferred to our leadership in the Dominican Republic and in the United States.

10. JJP: Which are the main generational changes and challenges in the political perspectives of old and new leaders?

   GL: Technology is probably the biggest challenge. In my trajectory, we were more engaged in hand-to-hand combat because digital technology was not there, and we had to deal with books. But now technology in small devices that are computers are eyes to the entire universe and everything that surrounds and impact us. Also, there is a widening gap between our children and how challenged parents are with all that they have to face nowadays: the cost of living, two jobs, the breakup of families, a system driven by capitalist interests that has widened the gap between the rich and the poor. We are wiping out the middle class as it used to exist at the beginning of the century and the 1970s and 1980s, and that meant that you could buy a home and a car, have vacations, pay attention to your kids, and take them to do things that were meaningful to shape their lives and made them savvier. Today, it is not the norm but an exception to see kids graduating from high school and entering college, and we see that many of them are unable to finish a degree. The challenges of today require us to be creative using technology but also to not lose sight that this is a struggle for humanity, communities, for family; and this is a struggle that is global. You need to have the sense of history, culture, and a global consciousness of your experience to continue to struggle to improve your condition as an individual and as part of the family, the community, the state, your home country, and humanity.

11. JJP: What are the future prospects for the Dominican American political empowerment in the U.S.?

   GL: I see a bright future for the young people that are emerging in leadership roles, both in the public and the private sector. They have gone to college, they have the experience, they acknowledge their background, their history, their commitment is there, and they have more opportunities now to coalesce and unite around. This is a great prospect that we have among young Dominican professionals. They have the opportunity to build coalitions with other ethnicities without which we cannot overcome all the challenges that we have. They can also forge a long-range agenda to help elevate the young people in the Dominican Republic. Education is a great equalizer but not only formal education.

Education is knowing where you are, to be grounded regardless of whether you have a college degree or not. If you bring the right approach in helping to extend a hand, just like others have helped you in your journey, that is the most powerful thing that you could do to legitimize yourself and help legitimize others. And also make sure that you leave that door open for those who are following in your steps, and they extend their hands to help others move along. I am very optimistic because my faith is with the people. That's what has driven me all the way to where I am today.

Figure 4.3 Councilmember Ydanis Rodriguez calls for Police Commissioner Ray Kelly's resignation. Credits: Eric McGregor. Flickr.

Interview with Former New York City Councilmember Ydanis Rodríguez

Ydanis Rodríguez was first elected to represent District No. 10 in the New York City Council in 2009 and was reelected in 2013 and 2017. During his tenure as councilmember, he served as Chair of the Transportation Committee for twelve years. He is one of the longest serving elected officials in the history of the Dominican American community in the United States. Following his tenure in the City Council, Mayor Eric Adams appointed him as New York City Commissioner of the Department of Transportation in December 2021.

During my interview with Commissioner Ydanis Rodríguez on October 29, 2023, via Zoom, I asked him the following questions:

1. JJP: When and how did you start your political career? Detail the main characteristics of your leadership? Please indicate your position(s), role(s), person(s) with whom or for whom you've worked.

YR: I am the result of the Liberation Theology Movement that emerged in the 1960s. I was influenced by my older sister, Zoila Ludovina Rodríguez, who was the first in my working-class family to embrace the cause for social justice as part of a group of young people who embraced the cause of the Liberation Theology Movement in the Dominican Republic.

I came to the United States in 1983 as a young man and I brought with me some organizing experience as a former member of the leftist political organization Dominican Patriotic Union (i.e., Unión Patriótica—UPA), the National Revolutionary Student Union (Unión de Estudiantes Revolucionarios—UNE), the Boy Scouts that was mostly composed by upper and middle-class youngsters, and the progressive Catholic youth organization Juvenile Pastoral (i.e., Pastoral Juvenil). While in the United States, I joined Radhamés Rodríguez (a.k.a. Radhamés Pérez) and Juan Villar from the leftist Dominican Labor Party (i.e., Partido de los Trabajadores Dominicanos—PTD). I worked as a high school teacher for fifteen years and a New York City councilmember for twelve years and was co-founder of the Gregorio Luperón High School. During those years,

I advocated for the freedom of Nelson Mandela, against the apartheid regime in South Africa, for the struggle of Rigoberta Menchú in Guatemala, to remove the U.S. Navy out of Vieques in Puerto Rico, and to stop police brutality in New York City. In addition, I worked in the organization of the students' takeover at City College in 1989 and 1991 for the establishment of free tuition and against budget cuts. My style has always been based on inclusion, from those early years as an activist and a teacher, up to my position as a city legislator, and now as commissioner of the world's largest transportation system. I manage an agency composed by almost 6,000 employees, with a capital budget plan of $37 billion dollars for ten years and $1.3 million dollars in expenses every year.

Many people influenced my understanding and value of inclusionary management that does not focus on personality and is based on results. As the Commissioner of Transportation, I believe, as well as Mayor Adams, in equity and that my work is not only about cars, roadways, and bridges. This department oversees 27% of the estate in New York City, and we have a department of arts through which I am pushing the agency to create opportunities for local artists by bringing exhibitions to public spaces. Following on my belief in inclusion and equity, I am committed to advance the conditions of the working and middle classes. Also, I understand that as our community has different levels of socioeconomic development, we need to work more toward crime prevention, taking into consideration the particular characteristics of every neighborhood.

2. *JJP:*   Which are the most important aspects of your personal experience as a political leader, including your main challenges and accomplishments?

YR: The challenges that I see are always linked to the everyday fight that people of color still have to go through. Segregation is not over; therefore, people of color are still at disadvantage, and I take this challenge as an opportunity for me and many others elected and appointed officials, and academics in the public sector, to push ourselves and use our positions not to be the only

Latinos, people of color, or women in those places, but to create similar opportunities for everyone who has been left behind in our society.

I am currently leading the Department of Transportation not because I am a Latino, although it is great to represent the Latino community as the first Latino and the second person of color running this agency, with the largest and most complex transportation system in the 350 square miles of New York City and 8.6 million people, and that oversees over 800 projects. We are organizing our streets to try to change the culture, so that people stop believing that the streets are only useful for those who drive cars but also for people to walk and ride a bicycle, as well as for art, entertainment, and summer activities.

3. *JJP:*   What have been the main challenges for Dominican American political leaders in their struggle for scarce political positions?

YR: We are still a group of people who have had to fight very hard to have access to mainstream positions and to be seen in a balanced way for our contributions at different levels; and it happens not only in politics but in academia, business, and media. Sometimes, we are so few in so many areas that we know who we are in different institutions, and this means that the almost one million Dominican inhabitants of New York City don't have enough opportunities. I am proud to say that I am working now in the same building that in 1988 I used to work in making sandwiches, and that despite my strong English accent, I have the values and skills to manage a strong entity.

My challenges are the same as with all Dominicans: the numbers that we represent in the city's population are not reflected in the leadership positions. Latinos represent 28% of New York City's population and we [Dominicans] are the second largest group, African Americans make up 24%, and Asians 15%. Those numbers are real, and they should be used in the formula to select who will be running different institutions. We come from working and middle-class families, and our struggles as Dominican Americans are to let society realize that we are not newcomers. As the CUNY Dominican Studies Institute and the Historical Society found out, there were four thousand Dominicans that came to New York City through Ellis Island in 1887 and Juan Rodríguez became the first non-Indigenous person who settled in what eventually became New York City in 1613. In my family that came for the first time in the 1960s, there are three generations that were born and raised here in the United States. And still, we are too far from being recognized as a group of people that make almost 8% of New York City's population and that demands and deserves the same opportunities that every other population in society gets.

4. *JJP:*   Mention important aspects of your personal experience (challenges and accomplishments) as a prominent Dominican American political leader.

YR: We must continue maintaining and expanding a coalition of all of us. People in government, both elected and appointed officials, work for the private sector, for academia, and for the rest of the people, but political figures, particularly those who decide to compete for reelection every two years, are the ones who people criticize the most even though both the private and public sectors are part of the same machine. There are public leaders like Espaillat and Ydanis, but there also many of us, such as Feniosky Peña Lora who is the Dean of Engineering and Science in Monterrey, the larger school of engineering in Mexico. He was the Edwin Howard Armstrong Professor of Civil Engineering and Engineering Mechanics and Professor of Computer Science at Columbia University and then served as the New York City Commissioner of the Department of Design and Construction. For me, Feniosky is a leader that has the same impact as an elected official, because as we know, there are no other political settlements like academic institutions. Also, last week, Quemuel Arroyo, former Chief Accessibility Officer and Special Advisor to the Chairman and CEO of the Metropolitan Transportation Authority (MTA), became the newest member of the Board of Trustees of New York University. Quemuel is a Dominican American who worked every day to make sure that MTA seeks communities that were left behind and identify how a new elevator could be installed to give the opportunity to people who are in disability to have access to the city, and that's politics. And we also have the artist Bony Ramírez whose work "Tropical" that has been displayed in several galleries around the world is now being exhibited in New York City.

Therefore, I believe that what we must keep doing is that once we see the talent that we all have not to give up, and when we see each other in the same space talk about our numbers, who we are, and how we can use that space in our society to create equal opportunity for everyone. I, myself, have supported others and elevated the role of elected officials in the twelve years that I represented Inwood because I never gave up on my agenda to provide affordable housing, create the People's Theater Project, and negotiate a 15,000 feet site for the Immigrant Resource Center for the Performing Arts in the rezoning process of Inwood.

I want my story to be the one of every single child, including newcomers from Latin America, Africa, and Ukraine. I am happy to realize that some of my former immigrant students from Gregorio Luperón High School have become teachers and have succeeded in other areas.

I believe society is a better place today because it has received from us the value of connectivity and we benefitted from those who facilitated this opportunity for us, as we have become facilitators for the new generation that will be playing the role of leaders in society and that I expect will be able to create new opportunities, especially for the disadvantaged ones.

5. *JJP:*   What were the main demands and needs of your constituents during your former position as Councilmember?

YR: The community asked for access to affordable housing, good education, jobs, public safety, and immigration reform. I understood that the community needed access to all these areas and that's why I did the Inwood rezoning, although there were big campaigns against it, with some saying that I was going to destroy the community, particularly when launching new projects such as building a new library. I had to patiently explain to the community that the old library needed to be demolished in order to build a new one that would be a fourteen-floor library building, with 175 affordable apartments at the top, and an art gallery for community artists, such as the building at 135 Riverside Drive where Ofelia García directed the Río Gallery in Washington Heights.

Also, another priority was to fight crime, for which I had to fight against police brutality and the officers that were involved in it. In addition, I had to push hard against those people who opposed policing the community, and I worked on building relationships between the police and the community. I put a lot of effort into giving a voice to the community; thus, every year in the month of January, I presented my state of the district report, in order to make myself accountable to the people. Every year, I invited all community-based organizations to provide them with information about the budget process. Also, I provided financial support to all the institutions in Northern Manhattan. I fulfilled my duties with transparency, participation, and support, which helped me get reelected.

6. *JJP:* What are the main demands of New Yorkers in your current position as Commissioner of the New York City Department of Transportation?

YR: As a commissioner, I address equity not from my desk, but from the perspective of a community that has never been heard. Some of the things that I have done include improving the benefits of minority- and women-owned business enterprises (MWBEs). Before I became a commissioner, only 11% of the contracts went to women and minorities; in my first year, I increased this number to 21%. In addition, I worked to increase diversity in the Department of Transportation (DOT). I support retention, but when there are any spaces vacant, I make sure that they are occupied by workers from the different ethnic and racial groups inhabiting New York City.

I have to think every day about the best way for our streets to move people and goods appropriately, and how to change the culture of working-class people, so that instead of embracing the wrong belief that cars are a symbol of progress and the only essential means of transportation,

and bikes are a symbol of poverty, they start appreci-
ating biking, that today is been seen as a transportation
means for only upper-middle-class educated individuals.
Thus, we want to share with the interfaith community, the
churches, the synagogues, and the temples the benefits of
biking and walking.

Transportation is something that we have not talked
about a lot. As art, it has been exclusive to middle-and
upper-class people who know the importance of joining
the planning division of DOT because they want to be the
coolest people that do the great jobs thinking about ideas
to create new plazas and free-access summer spaces and
trick or treat streets. I use my previous experiences from
the Caribbean and New York City to bring the conversation to my team and challenge progressive New Yorkers
who live in the Upper West Side, the Upper East Side,
Riverdale, and downtown Brooklyn to expend time with
me in underserved communities. I ask them: What do you
understand when you hear the word transportation? How
do you know that transportation impacts your life?

7. *JJP:*   Which are the main factors contributing to the evolution of
the Dominican American leadership and your role in the
development of the community's political empowerment?

YR: For me, it is about respecting the contributions of
everyone. I think that there is a generation of people like
you, Ramona Hernández, Silvio Torres-Saillant, Julissa
Reynoso, Junot Díaz, Yrthya Dinzey Flores, Carmen De
La Rosa, Guillermo Linares, Quemuel Arroyo, Feniosky
Peña Mora, and many others that encompasses a large
group of people that is very influential in the institutions
that we are related to. And its importance lies in how this
network has been able to have an impact on the community.
People like you, it doesn't matter where you are, whether
at John Jay College or Bronx Community College, I know
that everyone looks at Jacqueline Jiménez Polanco as the
future person that will be leading the institution.

I feel that we as Dominican Americans are part of the
group of people that in the last fifty years have been able
to be consistent, and that is what is important to me. The
methods and how we work change and that will always

be the case in society, but we must always maintain who we are. I was influenced by other people who came before me, and I am committed to bring equal opportunity for everyone, and I have been doing that in every position that I have occupied. For me is not how fast you run but about how you get to that mountain of social justice that Martin Luther King, Jr. said that we need to build, and that will be a reference for all members of society. We have a limited time regarding how long we will live, so for me it is about learning as Dominican Americans to pursue a lifestyle where we support each other.

8. *JJP:* Which are the main generational changes and challenges in the political perspectives of old and new leaders?

YR: One of the main challenges is to learn how to be inclusive and see the values and contributions of others that have different ideas than us. I learned in the 1990s from José González Espinosa, the founder of "Línea Roja" in the Dominican Labor Party (i.e., Partido de los Trabajadores Dominicanos—PTD), that being a revolutionary today is not to have a weapon, it is to bring ideas that other people should entertain.

9. *JJP:* What is the nature of the relationship between Dominican American leaders and Dominican political leaders in the island?

The most influential Dominican families, including the Vicinis, Rainieris, Corripios, Lamas, Thomens, and Rizeks, were working-class people who relocated in the island about 150 years ago and became role models to the Garcías, Rodríguezes, and Pérezes. Most of the people, like you and I, and others at the professional levels, at some point saw themselves or their parents going to school with nothing. I walked many miles and didn't have food when I went to school in the Dominican Republic, but I represent the story of most professional Dominicans and Dominican Americans who now are holding prestigious positions. In the last fifty to seventy-five years, as the result of movements fighting for democracy, we have turned ourselves into a group of individuals that are a reference here in New York City and back in the island for future generations of Dominican Americans and for other New Yorkers. There is no New York City without Dominicans and Latinos nor without people from over 150 countries. We are privileged to live in a city in which we can enrich ourselves through the values of different cultures. We endure racism and discrimination every day but we're a resilient people. Therefore, the relationship between us and those back in the island will always be a productive and respectful one. Dominican Americans contribute a lot to the leadership back in the island, now it is all about how we can help to run a society in the Dominican Republic that provides equal opportunity for everyone.

10. JJP: What are the future prospects for the Dominican American political empowerment in the U.S.?

YR: We need to "seguir trabajando duro" (continue to work hard). It is not about saying, "I have this knowledge and I have to be elected," we have to "sudar, remangarse, trabajar duro con la comunidad" (sweat, roll up one's sleeves, work hard with the community) and be connected with working-class people, not by bringing policies from a desk, but by going to the community. And I see this is being done by members of the new generation, such as New York City Councilwoman Pierina Sánchez, who graduated from Harvard and Princeton, and used to work for the Deputy Mayor of Economic Development; Councilmember Shawn Abreu and all members of the new generation of elected officials who do not have to speak Spanish to take to their hearts the fight for Dominican Americans and all New Yorkers. We have three or four generations of Dominican Americans who were born or raised here that decided to continue becoming involved in organizing the community instead of earning hundreds of thousands of dollars in the private sector. I am an optimist regarding the Dominican American community; we have gone very far in the last few decades and have been able to establish ourselves as a group of people that demand and earn respect, although there are a lot of glass ceilings to break.

Figure 4.4 Councilwoman Carmen De La Rosa. Credits: Felton Davis. Flickr.

Interview with New York City Councilwoman and Former New York State Assemblywoman Carmen De La Rosa

Carmen De La Rosa assumed office as a New York City council-woman on January 1, 2022, to represent District No. 10. In the past, she had occupied the position of New York State Assemblyperson for District No. 72 from January 1, 2017, to December 31, 2021. District No. 10 covers the northernmost neighborhoods of Manhattan, including Washington Heights, Inwood, and Marble Hill. The ethnic/racial population of the district is 81% Hispanic, 9% White, 6% Black, 2% Asian, and 1% other. Voter registration data shows that the district is composed of 77.2% Democrats, 5% Republicans, and 15.4% voters with no party preference.[2]

During my interview with Councilwoman De La Rosa on October 11, 2023, via Zoom, I asked her the following questions:

1. JJP: When and how did you start your political career? Detail the main characteristics of your leadership? Please indicate your position(s), role(s), person(s) with whom or for whom you have worked.

CDLR: I started my political career shortly after I graduated from college at Fordham University, with a bachelor's degree in political science and a concentration in Peace and Justice Studies in 2007. I was considering going to law school, but in the meantime, I applied for a few jobs and one of them led me to Assemblyperson Daniel O'Donnell's office in the Upper Westside, District No. 69 of Manhattan, for an interview. As soon as I got in, there was something I was familiar with: community. I saw beautiful blue walls with works from local artists and the office was full of people that needed help and assistance. I ended up working for Assemblymember O'Donnell for five years and I didn't go to law school. I worked as scheduler and community liaison providing services to the Spanish-speaking constituency that is mostly located in the part of the Upper Westside known as Manhattan Valley. I worked on legislation, education, and was able to learn how to write laws for the state. By the time I left his office, I was the district director.

Then, in 2010, I met former New York City Councilmember Ydanis Rodríguez and became his legislation and budget director for District No. 10. Then, I became his chief of staff and learned how to make, balance, and negotiate city budgets and how to write laws and legislate on behalf of the city. Meanwhile, I was doing political campaigns. I ran Ydanis' reelection campaign, and I was part of the team for Adriano Espaillat's campaign for congress in 2014.

In 2015, I ran for the honorary local position of female district leader in District No. 72 in the Democratic Party to try to get people civically engaged. Shortly after winning that position, I ran Espaillat's campaign for congress, and after he won, I was able to garner his support to run for a New York State Assembly seat. I ran against

Guillermo Linares and saw myself running against a historic figure who is also a Dominican. I won the seat and became the second Dominican American to be elected to the New York State Assembly. Besides becoming one of the few Dominican women holding an electoral position in New York, I ran because I wanted to be a voice for the younger generation of Dominican Americans that didn't see themselves reflected in politics as it was, and I identified with them because I was born and raised in the Dominican Republic and came to New York when I was a young girl. I ran with the commitment to build a bench of elected officials for Dominican Americans to continue to run for office. I won the position and became the second woman to be elected to the New York State Assembly in 2017 and I served for five years. In 2021, I ran for the New York City Council position that was vacated by Ydanis Rodríguez and became the first Dominican woman to hold that seat.

2. *JJP:*   Which are the most important aspects of your personal experience as a political leader, including your main challenges and accomplishments?

CDLR: One of the main aspects of my personal experience as an elected official is being a young woman of color in institutions that haven't had enough diversity in them. Here in New York, even though Latinos are one of the largest and fastest growing groups, we still don't have an adequate representation given the population and numbers that we hold, maybe because Latinos are not a monolith. I value the fact that I am representing a generation of New Yorkers that were raised here and had the experience of learning the English language as children in the city's educational system and who are working class, such as my mother who was a home attendant when I was growing up and my father who owned a grocery store in the Bronx. We didn't have a lot of means but we learned that community was at the center of everything we did. Thus, from an early age, my parents taught me that no matter my age or whether I am the first or the only one in the room, community comes first and is our responsibility to be the voice of that community at whatever table we seat. And I am taking that with me throughout my political career.

One of the many challenges that I have experienced is the issue of age. When I was first elected, I was in my early thirties, and I was always asked how old I was. I am thirty-seven years old now, and nowadays is when we see the uptake of younger elected officials, but back then, there was the notion that I was too young or inexperienced to hold the position or to make the decisions that I was making, even though I had already worked in government for over ten years.

Also, being a woman in a patriarchal society has also been a challenge. There have been times when I am campaigning for office and people say, "Where's your child?" or "Why you are not home taking care of your child?" Those are comments that are usually reserved for women; we don't hear that men are asked where their children are, it is assumed that they are with their mothers. Thus, pushing back against the norms of what young-elected officials should look like or dress like, or how they should comport themselves, and how we advocate and show up for our community, has been a challenge.

Sometimes, it is also difficult finding that you are the only one in the room, you are the only Latina, the only woman, the only one from Washington Heights representing all these generations of people that have been left behind. It is challenging to see yourself in those positions and having not sold out. Thus, fighting sell outs is something that I am very committed to, understanding that the position that I occupy is a position that I've earned because I've earned the trust of my community to make the decisions that represent them, and I have the confidence that I do what is the best for the people that I represent.

3. JJP: What are the main demands and needs of your constituents?
CDLR: I represent a high-need constituency from a community that is working class. The average median income in my community is approximately $50,000 a year (on the high end). A lot of the people that I represent are seniors that make less than $25,000 a year. Therefore, the high cost of housing and the displacement that is happening in

New York City are some of the main issues that come from my constituents. Also, being a representative in a multilingual and multi-ethnic community and make sure that my constituents feel informed whether they speak English, Spanish, or other languages is a challenge because our systems are not built to be equitable for people that do not speak English.

Most of the cases that come into my office have to do with issues around poverty, such as access to food and benefits like food stamps, housing, and immigration. Tenants in my district oftentimes must deal with being harassed and kicked out of their apartments, and the housing stock in my district is very old and doesn't have the infrastructure to accommodate large immigrant families. When it comes to immigration, there are mixed documented and undocumented families, as well as new arrivals and others who are waiting for the approval of their citizenship status to be able to vote and become civically engaged. I am working to make sure that people feel that they are engaged in the process even if they cannot vote yet.

4. *JJP:*   What are the main issues concerning the Dominican American political leadership?

CDLR: I am extremely proud as a Dominican for what we have accomplished in New York City; we are a small scrappy bunch. One out of every eight New Yorkers is a person of Dominican descent, and we are present in every state in the nation, including Alaska. In New York, we have one congressman, five state assembly members, and about six city councilmembers, as well as several judges (but we have no senators). Thus, we have some political representation, but we still don't have all the representation that we deserve.

Also, when we talk about what is the legacy that the Dominican leadership is going to leave to our people and how we preserve the integrity of Dominican neighborhoods as we contend with things like gentrification and displacement, this is a huge challenge and a concern. Traditionally, the heart of the Dominican diaspora in New York City has been Washington Heights, but now, most Dominicans live in the Bronx, thus we see how displacement plays out and that comes at a political cost.

In addition, when it comes to the empowerment of the younger generation, Dominicans need to become civically engaged. It is hard to convince people who are in the corporate sector or are not directly involved in politics to help with what happens in the community, of why it is so important to have their voices be a part of the political process.

5. *JJP:*   What are the main factors contributing to the evolution of Dominican American leadership and your role in the consolidation of the Dominican community's political empowerment?

CDLR: I am proud of being a Dominican woman despite the *machismo* that is present in our community, sometimes as a subconscious bias about the role of women. For example, the use of gender quotas in the Dominican Republic's political system is a direct reflection of us not seeing women in positions of power. I don't remember here in New York City who was that Dominican woman who has been granted a position of high power, but I have seen women who have been leaders in our community and those are the women that I look up to, and they are the people who have blazed the trail for me to become an elected official. But we don't have iconic Dominican females as political leaders here in the United States, we always go back to Mamá Tingó's or Anacaona's leadership in the island's history.

Thus, we need to open up spaces for women to have the right to be leaders of industries, executive directors, and deputy mayors. We now have Ana Almanzar as our first Dominican deputy mayor in New York City. We have started to turn around that narrative of political leadership to say, "hey, as Dominican women we are in power." Thus, if someone writes about the history of my career, I hope that they highlight that I am proud of being part of that first crop of female elected officials, so our daughters feel that they have Dominican female leaders that they can emulate in New York City's political society.

6. *JJP:*   Do Dominican American politicians endorse and are endorsed by politicians in the Dominican Republic? If so, how does this transnational collaboration work?

CDLR: Usually, we don't endorse candidates in the Dominican Republic's elections because the country has many political parties. I am a Democrat, and it is important for me to maintain the credibility of an American elected official and not pick a side in the political battles that are happening in the Dominican Republic, because the minute that I affiliate with a party in the Dominican Republic I am excluding people that I represent here in the United States.

It is important to have accountability and a voice in things that are playing out on a global scale. For example, here in New York, there are a lot of initiatives against domestic violence and we continue to see that *feminicidios* (femicides) are rising in number in the Dominican Republic, and as an elected official, it is important for me to highlight some of those things that are happening abroad without intervening in the processes that are occurring there, but instead using my platform to say "we see what's happening here and I want to be part of the solution for the problems back in our country."

7. JJP: What are the main challenges for Dominican American political leaders in their struggle for scarce political positions? How this affects the political empowerment of Dominican Americans?

CDLR: Some of the main challenges are displacement and gentrification in our communities. The Dominican vote is no longer as concentrated in clusters anymore. In the past, if you were a Dominican representing a community that was mostly encompassed by Dominicans, you were likely to get elected because *los dominicanos nos apoyamos unos a otros* (Dominicans support one another). But now the vote is not as concentrated as it was in the past because displacement has made it so that people had to leave the heart of the Dominican community, which was Washington Heights, and we see more Dominicans in Rhode Island, Pennsylvania, and New Jersey. That gives us the ability to have a more widespread representation but also the political block is not as concentrated.

Another challenge is the lack of financial resources for campaigns. Many of us, like it is in my case, come from working-class families. For example, when I first ran for the New York State Assembly seat, my parents asked how much the cost of a campaign was, and I said that my goal was to raise $100,000. They almost fell off their chairs and said, "*muchacha*, we have never seen this amount together, where we are going to get that money from?" That is the reality in our families, they don't have a large base of financial support because the little money that they manage to save is used to go back to the Dominican Republic or to take care of our grandparents there. Thus, it is a challenge for this new generation that comes to the political arena to learn how to fundraise and to put together the infrastructure needed for political campaigns.

8. *JJP:*   Which are the main generational changes and challenges in the political perspectives of Dominican American political leaders?

CDLR: One of the main generational changes and challenges is that there is a generational divide. My father, for example, grew up in the era of the dictatorship, when things were more mixed when it came to church and state. As Dominican Americans, we have had the luxury of democracy. Thus, for example, here as a Democrat, I am able to have open conversations about a woman's right to choose. In the Dominican Republic, that is something that is still up for debate. Thus, ideologically, generations have difficult experiences interacting with what happens back on the island.

I identify myself as a progressive Democrat, thus my views are left leaning and more connected with the most populous message saying that we need to make sure that we are providing health care, access to education, dignified housing, and that immigration laws take into account the migratory experiences of New Yorkers. I have the luxury of doing that in the tents of the Democratic Party, but when we have this conversation with older generations that came from a different political ideology, there is a disconnect. Thus, how we keep true to our traditions without offending those elder voters who were brought up in a completely different system than we were is a challenge.

9. *JJP:*   When and how did you start your connection with the Democratic Party?

CDLR: The first time I registered, I chose "no party preference," but as soon as I started working, I identified myself as a Democrat, and it happened organically.

10. JJP: How has the relationship between the Dominican American community and the Democratic Party developed?

CDLR: All of the Dominican American elected officials that I know in New York City and New York State are Democrats and we all have democratic values, but there are variations. As I said, I consider myself to be a progressive Democrat. If there is a framework of Democrats, there are right leaning, moderate, and progressive Democrats. In New York, we tend to skew from moderate to left, but there are variations even in that.

11. JJP: What have been the main challenges for Dominican American leaders to gain the recognition of the Democratic Party and occupy party positions?

CDLR: The Democratic Party has welcomed us with open arms, but something that sets us apart from other groups is that we have been very good at understanding how politics operate in our communities, and we have been able to rely on each other and support one another to climb up. As a working-class people, we identify with the values of the Democratic Party, and our elected officials are making sure to keep themselves true to those democratic values.

12. JJP: What are the prospects for the Dominican American political empowerment in the U.S.?

CDLR: When we talk about women that have been elected, we say that they broke the glass ceiling. I believe the glass ceiling is the ceiling before we hit the real ceiling because there is so much beyond that. I was born in the Dominican Republic, and I have a daughter that I am raising here. I can't be president because I wasn't born here, but my daughter can, and other colleagues can. We have our first congressman, and we need a U.S. senator. The Dominican political class that is in place right now sees the sky as the limit for people to continue to climb up. I can imagine a future with more Dominicans representing those states that have a large Dominican population. There is a real opportunity for us to be represented at the national level as well.

Figure 4.5 Senator Ana Quezada. State of Rhode Island General Assembly.

See www.rilegislature.gov/senators/quezada/Pages/Biography.aspx

Interview with Rhode Island State Senator Ana Quezada

Ana Quezada assumed office as Rhode Island State Senator on January 3, 2017, to represent District No. 2 that covers Providence. The ethnic/racial composition of her district is 76.2% White, 9.49% Hispanic, 4.04% Black, 3.24% Asian, 2.48% Native Hawaiian and other Pacific Islander, and 3.08% multiracial. Voter registration data shows 48% Democrats, 30% Republicans, and 22% voters with no party preference[3] (Ballotpedia, Data USA, Pew Research Center).

During my interview with Senator Ana Quezada on October 6, 2023, via Zoom, I asked her the following questions:

1. JJP: When and how did you start your political career? Detail the main characteristics of your leadership? Please indicate your position(s), role(s), person(s) with whom or for whom you've worked.

AQ: I came to the United States in 1982 to Terry Town, New York, and in 1990 I moved to Rhode Island and started participating in community advocacy and helping other Dominicans to get elected. I never even thought to run for politics myself. At that time, the Dominican community in Rhode Island was very active. I started helping my friend Leon Tejada by canvassing in his campaign for State Representative for District 11, knocking on doors and making phone calls. Tejada was the first Dominican State Representative elected in Rhode Island, and he was then elected as a councilmember. Afterward, I worked for the campaign of Angel Tavarez, who ran for mayor in Providence. I also helped in the campaigns of several other elected officials, Dominicans as well as non-Dominicans.

2. JJP: Which are the most important aspects of your personal experience as a political leader, including your main challenges and accomplishments?

AQ: I've been in politics for eight years and I have been a Senator for District No. 2 for the last seven years. My accomplishments include the passing of legislation that benefits our community, such as raising the minimum wage to fifteen dollars, medical insurance coverage for doulas as many of our women have low incomes and cannot pay for doulas out of pocket, control cameras in the state, driver licenses for undocumented immigrants, and also laws to protect interpreters in courts and homeowners from foreclosure. I am the Democratic Party's deputy majority leader in the State Senate. My main challenge is the English language, because as it is my second language and it has been hard for me, particularly at the beginning of my career, to be able to express myself with a vocabulary similar to that of my counterparts.

3. JJP: What are the main demands and needs of your constituents?

AQ: My constituents call me asking for jobs, assistance with different state and city departments, help with school issues, and housing.

4. JJP: What are the main issues concerning the Dominican American political leadership?

AQ: My main concern is the lack of voting turnout from the Latino community as they don't think it is important to come out and vote. We need to get them more involved; in particular, I want to see more young Dominicans participating in politics and voting, as they are less engaged than the elderly. Also, education is a big issue for our community. Sometimes, parents, due to their lack of English skills and the kind of jobs they do in factories, they don't get too involved in their children's education and school absenteeism is very high. Also, some parents make their older kids responsible for the younger ones and that affects their access to education.

5. JJP: What are the main factors contributing to the evolution of Dominican American leadership and your role in the consolidation of the Dominican community's political empowerment?

AQ: We need to be more empowered. We as a community are growing very fast in numbers, but we are not growing economically. Our Dominican immigrants come to this country and don't want to pay taxes, including businesses, and that affects our possibility to grow because they don't benefit from government programs and loans, such as the ones approved during the pandemic.

6. JJP: Do Dominican American politicians endorse Dominican Republic's candidates and are Dominican Americans endorsed by politicians in the Dominican Republic? If so, how does this transnational collaboration work?

AQ: The current president of the Dominican Republic, [Luis] Abinader, is putting a lot of interest on the engagement of the Dominican Republic's government with Dominican American elected officials. This is something that I didn't see in previous administrations. The Mayor of Lawrence [Massachusetts] organized a meeting between Dominican American elected officials and the government of the Dominican Republic, with the participation of over a hundred of us in a visit to the country during which we were received by President Abinader, the Senate's president, and the speaker of the House of Deputies. Among the attendees were many young U.S.-born Dominican Americans who are the children of elected officials and had never visited their parent's homeland, and this visit allowed them to get in touch with their roots and learn that we are Dominicans not by birth but by blood. This visit also motivated some recently elected Dominican American officials to make real estate investments in the country and apply for Dominican citizenship.

7. *JJP:* What are the main challenges for Dominican American political leaders in their struggle for scarce political positions? How this affects the political empowerment of Dominican Americans?

AQ: The biggest challenge that we have is the lack of economic resources to run for higher offices. For example, I ran for the U.S. Congress, and I couldn't make it due to the lack of financial endorsements.

8. *JJP:* Which are the main generational changes and challenges in the political perspectives of Dominican American political leaders?

AQ: We must work harder and become more united. I see that in the Dominican community as well as in other communities. Working together is hard.

9. *JJP:* When and how did you start your connection with the Democratic Party?

AQ: I started my connection with the Democratic Party when I got involved in politics. Before that, in 1995, I worked for the nonprofit organization John Hopes Settlement House, that mostly served the African American community, and that allowed me to see the needs of our community in areas such as education and housing. My connections with the Democratic Party started when I helped to run the reelection campaign of John McCauley for the Rhode Island State House of Representatives. One day, he said that I had a lot of charisma and that I should be thinking about running for office. He said that if one day he were leaving his seat, he would like for me to run for it. Then, I moved to another neighborhood and my state representative called me and asked to run for office. The first time

I ran for office was in 2010 for the state representative seat in District No. 10, and I lost. Then, I ran again, and I lost. Finally, I got elected as senator in November 2016.

We are Democrats, but the Democratic Party doesn't do a lot for us. The Latino community identifies as Democrats, but the Democratic Party takes advantage of the Latino community. They should be doing more because we are the base, and they need us, but they don't value us. We had a primary in the Democratic Party last September for the nomination of a candidate to the U.S. Congress and twelve candidates ran, including four African Americans, three Latinas (including me), and a Caucasian. The African American Gabe Amo won the election, and although I think that the Democratic Party will need us to get Amo elected in November, the party doesn't realize what we can do for them.

10. JJP: How has the relationship between the Dominican American community and the Democratic Party developed?

AQ: The relationship is good. Our State House Representative Grace Diaz is second in the Democratic Party and the first Dominican woman elected to the State House in Rhode Island. Juan Pichardo was the first Dominican elected to the State Senate in Rhode Island, and I am the first Dominican woman elected to the State Senate.

11. JJP: What have been the main challenges for Dominican American leaders to gain the recognition of the Democratic Party and occupy party positions?

AQ: I believe that the main challenge is the access to financial endorsements. Latinos and Dominicans don't provide financial endorsement to their leaders and that makes it difficult for us to run.

12. JJP: What are the prospects for the Dominican American political empowerment in the U.S.?

I hope that our youngsters understand the power of voting and getting politically involved.

Notes

1 See, https://en.wikipedia.org/wiki/Guillermo_Linares
2 See, https://en.wikipedia.org/wiki/Carmen_De_La_Rosa
3 See, https://ballotpedia.org/Ana_Quezada
   www.pewresearch.org/religion/religious-landscape-study/state/rhode-island/party-affiliation/   https://datausa.io/profile/geo/congressional-district-2-ri

5 Dominican American Political Activism in the Twenty-First Century

An Overview

In this chapter, I examine the main aspects of contemporary Dominican American involvement in U.S. politics. It will include an overview of current activism, the relationship between leaders and constituents, their main demands and criticisms, and the contributions of Dominican American politicians to American society. In addition, it will examine the future prospects of Dominican Americans in the U.S. electoral spectrum, considering their prominence as the fourth largest Latino/a/x population cohort and a significant political minority in New York City. I will also analyze what factors prevail in the Dominican American political engagement, including racial and ethnic issues and whether their main features contrast with or correspond to their early political involvement.

From the Shadows of Skyscrapers to the Halls of Congress

January 2017 marked the beginning of a new era for Dominican American political activism with the inauguration of Adriano Espaillat as the first Dominican-born U.S. Representative, followed by an increasing number of other Dominican American elected officials at the local and state level in the early 2020s. Historically relegated to the shadows of New York City's skyscrapers in poor and overcrowded neighborhoods, the Dominican American community struggled for decades to improve its socioeconomic conditions and become a part of U.S. mainstream politics. As pointed out by Tom Pérez, "Dominicans have not been in U.S. politics partly because previous generations were just starting to understand the American political system" (Ortiz 2023b). Pérez is a Senior Adviser to incumbent Pres. Joe Biden and

DOI: 10.4324/9781003497455-6

Table 5.1 Dominican-origin Population in the United States, 2020

Dominican-origin population	*Top states of residence (%)*
2,216,258	New York (40.5%)
	New Jersey (15.9%)
	Florida (12.2%)
	Massachusetts (7.3%)
	Pennsylvania (6.4%)
	Rhode Island (2.7%)
	Connecticut (2.3%)
	North Carolina (1.7%)
	Georgia (1.4%)
	Texas (1.3%)
	Maryland (1.2%)
	Other states (7.1%)

Source: Hernández, Rivera-Batiz, and Sisay 2022a, 9.

was Secretary of Labor in Pres. Barack Obama's administration; the first Dominican American to serve in a presidential cabinet position.

The Dominican American community has thrived gradually, although it is still politically underrepresented when one contrasts its population to the number of electoral positions, particularly at the U.S. congressional and senatorial levels. As shown in Table 5.1, the Dominican American population is largely concentrated in the East Coast (as of 2020), where it has most of its representatives. As seen in Table 5.2, all current Dominican American elected officials are Democrats and most of them have been elected at the county, city, and state levels, with only one federal representative in the House and no representation in the U.S. Senate. The largest representation is concentrated in New York with 48% of all Dominican American representatives, followed by Rhode Island with 21%. There is a small gap in gender representation, as 46% of elected Dominican American officials are women and 54% are men—which highlights the visible participation of Dominican American women in U.S. politics. Table 5.2 lists the names and elected positions of the forty-eight Dominican Americans that have been elected to county, city, state, and federal positions over the last decade (from 2013 to 2023). As shown in Figure 5.1, the representation of Dominican American elected officials is mostly concentrated in the state of New York with twenty-three positions (48% of total), followed by Rhode Island with ten

Table 5.2 Dominican American Elected Officials in the United States, 2013–2023

Years	Name & Party Affiliation	Position	City/County & State
2022–	Shaun Abreu (D)	Councilman	New York, New York
2017–2018	Marisol Alcántara (D)	State Senator	New York, New York
2023–	George Álvarez (D)	State Assemblyman	New York, New York
2016–2017	Daisy Báez (D)	State Representative	Miami, Florida
2008–2016	Alex Blanco (D)	Mayor	Passaic, New Jersey
2019–2023	Denis Bradley (D)	State Senator	Bridgeport/Stratford, Connecticut
2019–	Danilo Burgos (D)	State Assemblyman	Philadelphia, Pennsylvania
2022–	Fernando Cabrera (D)	Councilman	Bronx, New York
2011–	Carmen Castillo (D)	Councilwoman	Providence, Rhode Island
2009–2013	Nelson Castro (D)	State Assemblyman	Bronx, New York
2022– 2017–2021	Carmen De La Rosa (D)	Councilwoman, State Assemblywoman	New York, New York
2022–	Manny De Los Santos (D)	State Assemblyman	New York, New York
2021–	Brian De Peña (D)	Mayor	Lawrence, Massachusetts
2019–2023	Marcos Devers (D)	State Representative	Essex, Massachusetts
2005–	Grace Díaz (D)	State Representative	Providence, Rhode Island
2017– 2011–2016	Adriano Espaillat (D)	U.S. Congressman, State Senator	New York, New York
2018–2019	Aridia (Ari) Espinal (D)	State Assemblywoman	New York, New York
2019–	Pedro Espinal (D)	Councilman	Providence, Rhode Island
2014–2020	Rafael Espinal (D)	State Assemblyman	Brooklyn, New York
2022–	Amanda Farías (D)	Councilwoman	Bronx, New York
2019–	Antonio Felipe (D)	State Representative	Lawrence, Massachusetts
2021–	Leonela (Leo) Felix (D)	State Representative	Pawtucket, Rhode Island
2021–	Oswald Feliz (D)	Councilman	Bronx, New York

Year	Name	Office	Location
2009–2017	Julissa Ferreras (D)	Councilwoman	Queens, New York
2010–2014	William Lantigua (D)	Mayor	Lawrence, Massachusetts
2022–	Kendra Hicks-Lara (D)	Councilwoman	Boston, Massachusetts
2015–2016	Guillermo Linares (D)	State Assemblyman	New York, New York
2022–	Christopher Marte (D)	Councilman	New York, New York
2017–2019	Juana Matias (D)	State Representative	Essex, Massachusetts
2019–2021	Sabina Matos (D)	Lieutenant Governor	Providence, Rhode Island
2020–	Julia Mejía (D)	Councilwoman	Boston, Massachusetts
2018–	Pedro Mejía (D)	State Assemblyman	Hoboken, New Jersey
2007–	Joseline Peña-Melnyk (D)	State Delegate	Anne Arundel, Prince George, Maryland
2010–2018	José Peralta (D)	State Assemblyman	Queens, New York
2021–	Ramón Pérez (D)	State Representative	Providence, Rhode Island
2023–	Juan Pichardo (D)	State Senator	Providence, Rhode Island
2014–2021	Victor Pichardo (D)	State Assemblyman	Bronx, New York
2017–	Ana Quezada (D)	State Senator	Providence, Rhode Island
2023–	Estela Reyes (D)	State Representative	Essex, Massachusetts
2019–	Karines Reyes (D)	State Assemblywoman	Parkchester/Castle Hill, New York
2002–2013	Diana Reyna (D)	Councilwoman	Brooklyn, New York
2022–	Antonio Reynoso (D)	Borough President	Brooklyn, New York
2013–2014	Gabriela Rosa (D)	State Assemblywoman	New York, New York
2011–2014	Davian Sánchez (D)	City Council	Providence, Rhode Island
2022–	Pierina Sánchez (D)	Councilwoman	Bronx, New York
2021–	Yudelka Tapia (D)	State Assemblywoman	Bronx, New York
2011–2015	Angel Taveras (D)	Mayor	Providence, Rhode Island
2023–	Deni Taveras (D)	County Councilwoman	Prince George, Maryland

Sources: Ortiz (2023a), Matos and Morel (2021), Wikipedia https://en.wikipedia.org/wiki/Category:American_politicians_of_Dominican_Republic_descent

Note: (D) Democratic Party.

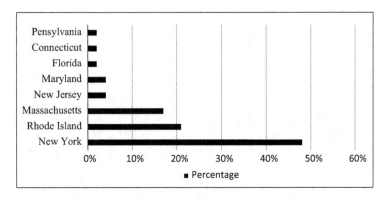

Figure 5.1 Dominican American Electoral Representation, 2013–2023.

Sources: Ortiz (2023a), Matos and Morel (2021). Wikipedia https://en.wikipedia.org/
wiki/Category:American_politicians_of_Dominican_Republic_descent

(21%); Massachusetts with eight (17%); New Jersey and Maryland with two each (4%, respectively); and Florida, Connecticut, and Pennsylvania with one each (2%, respectively). The current electoral representation of Dominican Americans has more than doubled in size since that of 2004 (as shown in Table 2.5).

As stated by Rhode Island State Lieutenant Governor Sabina Matos, Dominican Americans have advanced politically because they take chances: "they are willing to get in the political arena and put themselves out there" (Ortiz 2023a). Matos, who was backed by Adriano Espaillat, was one of two Dominican American women vying for the Democratic Party's nomination to represent Rhode Island in Congress in 2023. The other candidate was Rhode Island State Senator Ana Quezada, who was the first Dominican American woman elected to that position.[1] They were both eliminated in the Democratic primary, but if any of them had managed to win the nomination and the race, it would have been the first time that a Dominican American woman had gotten the opportunity to get a seat in the U.S. House of Representatives.

Although Rhode Island has a large Dominican constituency (some of them women) at the state and local levels, including one senator, three state representatives, three councilmembers, and one lieutenant governor, Matos and Quezada did not get nominated. It may seem like Matos and Quezada failed to get nominated because they split the Dominican American vote, but as Quezada stated,

> This was not an important factor because even if our votes were added to present only one candidate, we wouldn't have won. There were three Latinas competing for the same position and if we had added our votes to support one candidate, we wouldn't have won either. There was a tight competition between minority candidates and an African American won the nomination. Besides, competition between Dominicans or Latinos will be seen very often because the community is growing. The fact that there were two Dominicans and another Latina running, was highly criticized as many thought that we should have unified our vote so that only one ran, but even if we would have done that, we hadn't won this contest.[2]

The ascent of Espaillat to Congress and the growing representation of Dominican American politicians in the last decade have marked the difference between the past and the present of the Dominican American community's political activism. New York City Councilmember Oswald Feliz states that, from now on, everyone in the political realm of the Democratic Party, from the city to the state to the federal level, has started to pay attention to the Dominican American community, listening directly to the people and asking how they can be helpful.[3] This is an indicator of the community's political maturity, made possible by the capacity of senior leaders to mentor young ones and their overall ability to maintain a high level of coherence between contenders, despite their distinctive points of view. As pointed out by Lilliam Pérez, a long-term community activist and former chief of staff to State Senator and Attorney General Eric Schneiderman,

> when it comes to supporting a Dominican American candidate, rivalries are left aside as it happened when Adriano Espaillat supported his historical contender Guillermo Linares when he ran against the Jewish American Eric Schneiderman for the New York State Senate in 2002.[4]

Furthermore, Espaillat commended Linares on his appointment by Governor Andrew Cuomo to lead New York State Higher Education Services Corporation in 2017. Espaillat stated,

Guillermo Linares has a distinguished record in public service and has long served as a champion of education and ensuring quality and affordable education for New York students and their families. Guillermo will be a vital asset to New York's education system, and I look forward to continuing our work together to ensure access to quality higher education remains affordable and accessible for all New York students who desire to achieve.

(Adriano Espaillat 2017)

In addition, Dominican American politicians have proven their abilities to negotiate with diverse racial/ethnic sectors, as reflected in the strong alliance between Espaillat and Schneiderman that gained the Dominican American community the support of Jewish Americans, and the accomplishment of projects such as the Innocence Project to assist wrongly incarcerated people, and the construction of the Jewish Museum in Sosúa, Dominican Republic, to honor World War II European Jewish refugees sheltered by the Trujillo regime.[5] The alliance with Puerto Ricans has been important in the political empowerment of Dominican Americans in New York City, as the latter won positions that were previously occupied by Puerto Rican leaders (who in turn had gained them from Irish Americans). For example, the support of Puerto Rican leaders to Guillermo Linares has been key to his political success, among them, Luis Miranda, the first Latino Commissioner of New York and master of the political movement in Washington Heights who has preserved political links with the Dominican American community, and Assembly member Roberto Ramírez from the Bronx and Chair of the Bronx Democratic Party. Both Miranda and Ramírez have been backed by Irish Americans.[6]

Community work has been essential in the development and consolidation of Dominican American leadership. Initially organized through the Area Policy Boards (APBs) and the Community School Boards (CSBs), Dominican Americans were also able to get involved in politics by joining the Democratic Party state committees. Raysa Castillo, who was elected to a Community School Board, states that,

Dominicans became the lowest but the most active members of the Democratic Party state committees, that are the ones needed to collect signatures. Thus, these two forms of political involvement, the Community School Boards and the Democratic Party state committees, merged because the party was attracted by the people who were in the Community School Boards as they had the experience of organizing because both processes were the same.[7]

In addition, Dominican Americans have established solid grassroots organizations to push for their incorporation into the U.S. political arena, including Alianza Dominicana, Northern Manhattan Coalition for Immigrant Rights, the Dominican Women Caucus, the Dominican Women Development Center, the Dominican American National Roundtable, and Dominicanos USA (DUSA), among many others. Through naturalization, registration and voting campaigns, fundraising and donations, the Dominican American community has been able to gain the endorsement of the Democratic Party to political leaders competing for electoral positions. As pointed out by Lilliam Pérez,

The possibility of getting power is not given to a community because they inhabit in a particular state. The electoral positions need to be pushed. The least effort is done within parties; most of the work is done by community leaders. The Democratic Party asks the community about strong senior leaders, the amount of money collected, and the amount of people the community can move; fundraising and voter turnout are the main factors. Thus, the Dominican community organizes and raises money. The party needs to be pushed by the organized society that, in turn, needs to let the party know that the community is fulfilling those requirements. The campaign process includes petitions, collecting signatures, and getting them to the board of elections. The community needs to submit a legal number of signatures correctly to be able to run for election.[8]

This reflection exemplifies some essential components examined in this book, which has acknowledged the important contributions of the Dominican American community to the development of its political leadership. In a highly politicized immigrant community, in which political debates constitute a natural element of people's daily lives back in the homeland, a cultural value that is passed from older generations to new ones, forceful social activism in a pluralistic institutional environment has become the compelling rite of passage into U.S. mainstream politics.

Dominican Americans and Afro-Latino/a/x Identity

As Dominican American politicians have started to gain public influence, their racial and ethnic identity has raised the attention of the U.S. media. In an online survey conducted in 2021–2022 through communications sent to forty-nine Dominican American officials, out of twenty-eight respondents seventeen identified as Afro-Latino and eleven identified as Black. When asked whether their political future was bound to that of other Latinos/as/xs and African Americans, most Dominican American officials said they felt politically linked to both groups. The Afro- Latino/a/x ethnic/racial identity position is considered "useful in government coalition-building, which is necessary for any underrepresented U.S. group to achieve its goals." In addition, the report indicates that Dominican American elected officials "may be in a position to close the gap between Latino and African American coalitions at local and state levels," where most of them serve (Bueno Vásquez, Matos, and Morel 2022).

The racial and ethnic Afro- Latino/a/x identity is controversial for Dominican Americans in the political realm because many constituents identify primarily as Dominicans or Dominican Americans and do not dwell on their mixed-Black or African heritage, although it represents over 80% of the Dominican Republic's population. This apparent contradiction is linked to the historic identity formation of Dominicans as based on their ethnic or national identity, rather than on their racial heritage, on top of the ultra-conservative institutional neglect of most Dominicans as mixed-Blacks, Blacks, or Afro-descendants, a path inherited from the openly racist dictatorships of Rafael Trujillo (1930–1961) and Joaquín Balaguer (1966–1978). This tendency has gradually changed, as many Dominicans in the Dominican Republic nowadays demand the institutional recognition of their mixed Taíno and Black race, as well as the Dominican diaspora whose migratory processes have informed their perception about blackness, and many have embraced their African and Taíno heritage, too. And this change is also noticeable among the community's top political leaders, such as Adriano Espaillat, whose genuine embracement of his ethnic/racial identity as a Latino of African descent or Black and Latino has translated into great success for his political career, both as a contender and ally, and also as a mentor of a new generation of politicians.

For example, when reflecting about the main issues concerning the Dominican American leadership and the challenges they face in the struggle for scarce political resources, Raysa Castillo, a long-standing Afro-Dominican community activist, politician, political advisor, and prominent attorney at law, states that the main issues are how Dominican Americans identify themselves and whom they ally with. In this context, Castillo affirms,

> If we look at the highest-ranking Dominican politicians embodied by Adriano Espaillat, he exemplifies how the identity and inter-ethnic/racial alliances issues must be handled by Dominican Americans if they want to win an electoral position. When he unseated Irish American Assemblymember Brian Murtaugh he ran in a district mostly inhabited by Dominican Americans but primarily represented by Irish Americans and an African American minority. Espaillat won because he is a person of color who was able to represent Dominicans and also get on board African Americans. Espaillat was the right Dominican for that particular time. And he has been able to continue to handle this issue as he successfully ran for the New York State Assembly and the New York State Senate, and finally got to the U.S. Congress and defeated former African American Congressman Charles Rangel, who was a national and international figure, and this is a big accomplishment as he has had the ability to form alliances with African Americans and Jewish Americans.[9]

The racial/ethnic identity of Dominican American leaders and constituents is very important in a country like the United States, where nation building was based on centuries of African enslavement and the subsequent conflict between Whites and Blacks following the Civil War and the Jim Crow era. Dominicans, on the other hand, come from an island whose territory was the first settlement for African slaves in the early sixteenth century. However, the Dominican national state building was based on a postcolonial border conflict with Haiti in which the Dominican people's identity was established on an ethnic or national basis rather than a racial basis. The colonial division of the island between the eastern territory of Hispaniola (formerly known as Santo Domingo, then Spanish Santo Domingo, and finally the Dominican Republic) and Haiti, following the bloody war that allowed the independence of Dominicans from Haiti in 1844, created the basis for an institutional identity of Dominicans vis-à-vis their Haitian neighbors. Dominican Americans, as well as their compatriots in the Dominican Republic, are very aware of their African heritage as clearly manifested in their dark skin tones and their syncretic religious and cultural practices, but many have chosen to overlap it with their national/ethnic identity as "Dominicans" in order to claim a neat link to their small homeland that incorporates the nature of their diverse racial identity as a mixed people of mostly Taíno, Black, and White descent with other Asian and Middle Eastern minority components.

In the United States, Dominicans are pushed to identify themselves as Latinos (an ethnic term originally incorporated by Puerto Ricans in the United States), and in the meantime, some have failed to publically embrace their Black heritage since blackness is seemed as a privilege belonging only to African Americans, Africans, or other people of African descent whose native language is not Spanish. Therefore, when it comes to the political realm, politicians who identify as Afro-Latino/a/x, Black and Latino/a/x, or Latino/a/x of African descent are welcomed by Latino/a/x groups but rejected by Black groups. For example, despite his determination and clear ethnic and racial identity as a Latino of Black or African descent, Adriano Espaillat was denied membership in the Congressional Black Caucus. Espaillat's reaction to that rejection is expressed in his statement when he says,

> I am persistent and I will continue to knock on the door because I don't think someone else has the right to define my Blackness or to determine whether I am a Black or not. I mean, I don't have to take a DNA test or go to Ancestry.com to tell someone. Someone should not hold me to that standard, so I will continue to knock on the door. Maybe it's a political thing because I replaced a giant person, Charlie Rangel, but I am now the representative of Harlem for the last six years, and I deserve to be a member of the Black Caucus and will continue to push for that battle.
>
> (Allasan 2022)

The rejection of Espaillat by the Congressional Black Caucus reflects how Dominican Americans are misperceived at the racial level by African Americans. The fact that Dominicans speak Spanish automatically places them in the Latino/a/x or Hispanic community, a misperception by many U.S. Americans which to them means that Dominicans are not Black. An obliviousness that is linked to misinformation about the history of Latin America and the historical presence of Africans and people of African descent in the Spanish Caribbean, Central and South American territories well before their transatlantic passage to North America. On the other hand, Dominicans who arrived in the United States in the 1960s had been culturally indoctrinated by the long-standing Trujillo dictatorship to fear expressing their political ideas and openly embracing their African heritage, something that permeated the minds of many who witnessed the atrocities against Trujillo's opponents and the 1937 massacre of Haitians and Dominicans of Haitian descent in the borderlands.

When talking about the border conflicts, Paulino (2016) stated that Trujillo created a safeguard zone in the Haitian-Dominican borderlands through the establishment of state institutions and the launching of an ideological campaign against what was considered an intrusive Black, inferior, and bellicose Haitian state. I argue that because during the Trujillo dictatorship Dominicans were forced to identify themselves as non-Blacks, some members of the early Dominican diaspora arrived in the United States afraid to openly advocate for their own blackness, although they widely nurtured the Afro-Dominican cultural and religious values that were censored during Trujillo's racist regime and the succeeding pro-White Hispanic institutions established by Balaguer that persecuted and oppressed people of color. Moreover, it was still latent in their memory the death of Haitians and Dominicans of Haitian descent during the infamous 1937 massacre.

Nevertheless, during liberal political periods of the nineteenth and twentieth centuries, before and after the Trujillo regime, Dominicans historically expressed their resounding political support for Black leaders, such as founding father Francisco del Rosario Sánchez, who was interim president and president of the Central Government Board in 1844 (i.e., Junta Central Gubernativa), following the independence from Haiti, and governor of Santo Domingo (1856–1858). Another prominent Black military figure was Gaspar Polanco, who was president of the Dominican Republic from 1864 to 1865, following the Restoration War against the annexation of the Dominican Republic by Spain. Also, Dominicans venerate the paradigmatic figure of Gregorio Luperón who fought in the Restoration War and became vice president in 1865 and president from 1879 to 1980. Later on, Dominicans buoyed Ulises Heureaux (Lilís), a Black man of Haitian descent who governed the country during two presidential terms as a liberal from 1882 to 1887 and as a conservative caudillo from 1887 to 1889.

In the modern era, the Black leader José Francisco Peña Gómez was one of the most prominent and popular political figures of the twentieth century in the Dominican Republic. Peña Gómez, who was the son of Haitian parents who were victims of the 1937 massacre, was the top leader of the major Dominican Revolutionary Party (i.e., Partido Revolucionario Dominicano, or PRD), from 1973 until his death in 1998. He was also mayor of Santo Domingo (1982–1986) and a presidential candidate on three occasions (1990, 1994, and 1996) (Jiménez Polanco 1999). At the grassroots level, Dominicans worship the figure of the rural Black female leader Florinda Muñoz Soriano, popularly known as Mamá Tingó, who was murdered in 1974 by a powerful landowner during Balaguer's authoritarian regime for her defense of the land rights of poor peasants.

At the cultural level, Dominicans and Dominican Americans have overcome the legacy of Trujillo's and Balaguer's racism, as they have had access to a more pluralistic and sophisticated intersectional education. And Rep. Adriano Espaillat, as well as other Dominican American politicians who have been participating in the U.S. political arena since the 1980s and 1990s, have become part of that cadre of Dominican politicians who candidly embrace their *negritud* (blackness). In addition, Dominican American community organizations such as the Dominican Day Parade, Alianza Dominicana, Dominican Women's Caucus, and the Dominican Women's Development Center have played an important role in enlightening the U.S. community about the Dominican African heritage and its intersection with gender and ethnic issues. The great contributions of the CUNY Dominican Studies Institute (DSI) to the spread of narratives about the historical presence of Blacks in the Dominican Republic through the peculiar research, exhibit, and digital platform "First Blacks in the Americas" that disseminates the history of the early inhabitants of Black/African ancestry of the Dominican Republic is noticeable as well.[10] The essence of this analysis is summarized by Raysa Castillo, when she states,

> Dominicans in the U.S. are pushed to act as a group and embrace the idea that we are all the same. The U.S. majority incorporates the idea that Dominicans are just a minority and that becomes challenging for the older generation because their lives are dedicated to what they have, that is the identity of where they are from. Generations subsequent to the initial migrant generation see

themselves as different and want to be counted as who they really are, as Black-Latino-Dominicans.[11]

Undeniably, members of the new generation of Dominican American politicians connect with the multiple identities of their constituents and claim they are entitled to a Dominican American Afro-Latino/a/x or African identity, such as the case of former New York Councilwoman Julissa Ferreras, who identifies herself as the first person of color and the youngest member to be elected chair of the Finance Committee in Brooklyn.[12] Also, there is the case of Rhode Island State Representative Leonela Felix, who serves as co-chair of the Rhode Island Black, Latino, Indigenous, Asian-American and Pacific Islander Caucus (RIBLIA).[13] In addition, Rhode Island Lieutenant Governor Sabina Matos identifies herself as the first Black female statewide officeholder in Rhode Island.

What Do Dominican American Voters Want?

In 2021, Dominican Americans represented the fourth largest Latino/a/x community in the United States, along with Cubans (Pew Research Center 2023). Dominican American voters are mostly concentrated in New York, New Jersey, Florida, Massachusetts, Pennsylvania, and Rhode Island (as shown in Table 5.1). In interviews with Dominican American officials, they expressed that the main demands of their constituents are issues related to poverty that include good jobs, education, housing, immigration reform, and health care. These demands are reflected in the results of a survey

Table 5.3 Main Issues for Dominican American Voters (2015)

Most important issues politicians should address	*Percentage*
Create more jobs	29%
Improving schools and education reform	23%
Cost of housing and cost of renting	20%
Immigration reform and immigrant rights	13%
Access to health care	7%
Discrimination against Latinos	5%
Lower taxes	5%
Issues related to policing	4%

Source: Dominicanos USA (DUSA) 2015, 2.

conducted by Dominicans USA (DUSA), as shown in Table 5.3. When asked what were the most important issues that Dominican communities face in their cities that politicians should address, most of the interviewees indicated jobs, education, housing, immigrants' rights, and access to health care. Other issues included discrimination, high taxes, and policing.

These concerns have become particularly salient following the effects of the Coronavirus pandemic in the Dominican American community and other communities of color, particularly those located in overpopulated urban settlements, where the estimated mortality rates were just 0.03% for non-Hispanic Whites, but 0.18% for non-Hispanic Blacks and 0.12% for Hispanic adults (Hernández, Ortega, Sohler, and Marrara 2022b).

These mortality rates reflect the socioeconomic conditions of Dominican Americans, who had a median annual personal earning of $30,000 for those aged sixteen and older in 2021, the same as it is for the overall Latino/a/x population. This indicates that the average income earnings for Dominican Americans have increased since 2019 when it was just $22,551, compared with the overall U.S. population's median income of over $36,000 (as examined in Chapter 2). The U.S. Census Bureau indicates that 20% of Dominican Americans live in poverty compared to 18% of Latinos/as/xs. In addition, the possibility to move up the socioeconomic ladder into the U.S. middle class is limited for Dominican Americans and the overall Latino/a/x population as only 22% of Dominican Americans obtained at least a bachelor's degree in 2021, compared to 20% of Latinos/as/xs. In addition, homeownership rates for Dominican Americans are very low; only 31% of Dominican Americans are homeowners, compared to 51% of Latinos/as/xs. Moreover, many Dominican Americans still face the challenge of learning the English language, as the proficiency for adults is just 55%, compared to 67% for Latino/a/x adults (Pew Research Center 2023).

Therefore, many Dominican voters in New York City do not represent the average middle-class homeowner. For example, New York Councilwoman Carmen De La Rosa states that 70% of the issues raised by her constituents in Washington Heights are related to housing and many of them are poor Spanish-speaking seniors who earn a low annual income of less than $25,000. She explains that gentrification and displacement are severely affecting many poor Dominican Americans who are forced to leave Manhattan and relocate to impoverished areas in the Bronx and other cities in the Northeast where rent is cheaper.[14] Housing affordability issues are critical for Dominican Americans, as many of them reside in metro areas with a high cost of living (like New York City) where people aged 22–34 spend over 40% of their income on rent (J. Weston Pipper 2015).

Rep. Espaillat believes that increasing the number of people attending school will improve the jobs and housing affordability situation, based on the socioeconomic equation from democratic capitalist societies that more education translates into a greater access to jobs and a higher capacity to cover up people's needs. He states that,

> When we get a lot of young students, and they come out as professionals, you're going to see the unemployment and jobs issue come down one slot—one position. I think education will also go up, because those folks will recognize that their achievements are directly connected to education. Housing will also be less relevant, because if you make more money, you're able to purchase your own home.
>
> (J. Weston Pipper 2015)

The overall theme of this chapter is the increased representation of the Dominican American community in U.S. politics and its intersection with a growing population, their racial and ethnic identity, and the particular needs of voters. This reflects some aspects that were analyzed regarding the political involvement of Dominican Americans in the past, particularly their demands for improved socioeconomic conditions that have prompted many to vote for the Democratic Party and its officials who represent the liberal and progressive ideas of the party. The new element in the political equation is the ethnic and racial issue component, which was not a basic component in the early political incorporation of Dominican Americans back in the 1980s and 1990s. This development obviously reveals a generational change that began with the victory of Adriano Espaillat over Charles Rangel's handpicked candidate Assemblyman Keith Wright for the U.S. Congressional seat to represent Harlem in 2016. Espaillat's victory, in turn, has sparked a discussion over Dominican and Dominican American African/Black identity that echoes the plea of a new generation that clearly embraces these ancestral values freely—unlike older generations—which ultimately is fostering a dialogue over ethnic and racial issues in a community where a traditional national or ethnic identity had superseded its racial identity.

Notes

1 Interview with Rhode Island State Senator Ana Quezada, October 6, 2023, via Zoom.
2 Interview with Rhode Island State Senator Ana Quezada, October 20, 2023, via WhatsApp.
3 Interview with New York City Councilman Oswald Feliz, October 3, 2023, via Zoom.
4 Interview with Lilliam Pérez, September 28, 2023, via Zoom.
5 Interview with Lilliam Pérez, September 28, 2023, via Zoom.
6 Interview with Lilliam Pérez, September 28, 2023, via Zoom.
7 Interview with Raysa Castillo, October 7, 2023, via Zoom.
8 Interview with Lilliam Pérez, October 5, 2023, via Zoom.
9 Interview with Raysa Castillo, October 7, 2023, via Zoom.
10 See,   http://firstblacks.org/en/summaries/spotlight-short-announcing-act ivation-of-website/
11 Interview with Raysa Castillo, October 7, 2023, via Zoom.
12 See, https://en.wikipedia.org/wiki/Julissa_Ferreras
13 See, www.rilegislature.gov/representatives/felix/Pages/Biography.aspx
14 Interview with New York Councilwoman Carmen De La Rosa, October 11, 2023, via Zoom.

Conclusion

The Political Empowerment of Dominican Americans in the Latino/a/x Spectrum

As examined in this book, Dominicans started their political activism in the United States with the national and international involvement of political exiles who had settled in New York and Florida in strategic and military actions against the U.S. military occupation of the Dominican Republic (1916–1924), the sultanistic Trujillo regime (1930–1961), and Balaguer's autocratic regime (1966–1978). Nevertheless, it was not until the 1980s that Dominicans and Dominican Americans got engaged in U.S. electoral politics and that involvement grew gradually until the present, making Dominican Americans a significant ethnic minority in the U.S. political arena. Some of the long-standing elected and appointed officials (such as Ydanis Rodríguez) were members of the Dominican Labor Party (i.e., Partido de los Trabajadores Dominicanos—PTD), a leftist organization from the Dominican Republic, when they took their first steps into U.S. politics. Moreover, other PTD leaders, some of whom were political exiles, were the political mentors of the Dominican American Generation X whose members encompassed the youth organization "Dominicans 2000." In addition, the traditional political parties of the Dominican Republic, such as the PRD (Dominican Revolutionary Party), PLD (Dominican Liberation Party), PR/PRSC (Reformist Party and Reformist Social Christian Party), PRM (Modern Revolutionary Party), and FP (Peoples' Force), have established branches in the United States, seeking votes and monetary support and sharing strategic experiences with the Dominican diaspora (although young Dominican American elected officials are not interested in seeking to strengthen relationships with the Dominican Republic's parties because they see that as counterproductive to their relationship with

DOI: 10.4324/9781003497455-7

their Dominican American constituency, due to the intense competition among Dominican political parties). Currently, there are seven overseas congress members (i.e., *diputados de ultramar*) representing the diaspora in the Dominican Legislature, including three from the United States, and all of them are from the PRM.

In the long term, Dominicans developed a strong community activism that started with their participation in the Area Policy Boards (APBs) and Community School Boards (CSBs) of the City of New York, a strategy that subsequently allowed the incorporation of activists into the Democratic Party's state committees through grassroots engagement. In doing so, Dominicans created a model of political participation that became paradigmatic in the Latino/a/x community, as the majority of those who initially engaged in political activism through the APBs and CSBs were undocumented immigrants and, consequently, could not vote in U.S. elections. Thus, the core work of political leaders consisted in fighting for the solution of socioeconomic issues and the naturalization and registration of their potential constituents, an effort that started in the 1980s and has persistently continued throughout the 1990s and the 2000s with the support of Dominican American elected officials and grassroots organizations. Indeed, there have been iconic moments during which *all* Dominican community organizations have taken a common stance toward the naturalization and registration of members of the community. For example, during the "Contract with America," a legislative plan launched by Republican Speaker of the House Newt Gingrich in 1994 to end welfare and other social benefits for non-U.S. citizens, and the 1996 Illegal Immigration Reform and Immigrant Responsibility Act passed during Bill Clinton's presidency to reinforce U.S. immigration laws and add penalties for undocumented immigrants who committed crimes while in the United States or remained in the United States for statutorily defined periods of time. This latter measure also included a threat to remove U.S. permanent resident status and increased deportations.

As detailed in this book, Dominicans share a very politically active lifestyle in their homeland that has driven migrants to join community associations during all facets of their diasporic experience in the United States—an important element to develop political engagement in the recipient country, as analyzed by U.S. Latino/a/x scholars. The novel element here is that, unlike the traditional political models of the Dominican Republic and the United States in which parties are the center of activism, the exclusionary hindrances faced by the Dominican diaspora have forced Dominican Americans in the United States to rely on community organizations to demonstrate to the U.S. party machineries that they are capable of mobilizing massive amounts of people, forging alliances with other ethnic/racial communities, and raising enough money to support potential candidates who could beat their competitors and win elections. And if Dominican Americans could not convince U.S. traditional parties about their competitive electoral skills, then they would run as independents, as William Lantigua, former state representative from Lawrence, Massachusetts, did in 2004. Until the early 2000s, Dominican American leaders played both sides of the political game running as candidates for both the Democratic and Republican parties. Since the last decade, however, all Dominican Americans elected officials represent the Democratic Party, as it epitomizes the core values and demands of their constituents that center around the struggle for social justice and equity, either from a moderate or a progressive perspective.

In the Latino/a/x political spectrum, Dominican Americans, who have been underrepresented in scholarly publications, could become a role model for gradually and continuously achieving electoral success, despite their historical migratory experiences as undocumented political actors and the English language-barrier challenges that they have faced—as has been thoroughly examined in this book through interviews with current electoral officials. On the other hand, Dominicans have built their political engagement in spaces left by other racial and ethnic minorities, including African Americans and Puerto Ricans, as well as White ethnics such as Jewish Americans and Irish Americans, that have opened the doors for Dominican Americans to become a part of U.S. mainstream politics. This trend also highlights the capacity of Dominicans to mingle, ally, and negotiate with diverse racial and ethnic groups: a byproduct of an inclusive Dominican racial identity that encompasses the diverse racial and ethnic legacy left by their Indigenous Taíno ancestors, the infamous European conquest, and the transatlantic African slave trade, as well as the different immigrant groups from all around the world that have settled in the Dominican Republic during postcolonial times.

In conclusion, this book brings to light the challenges, struggles, and contributions of Dominican Americans to the U.S. political realm as a means to encourage U.S. scholars and students to become more cognizant of Dominican American political activism and stimulate their intellectual curiosity for the development and political empowerment of Dominican Americans, Latinos/as/xs, African Americans, and other racial and ethnic minorities in the United States.

References

Alduey Sierra, José. 1992. "La defensa de los inmigrantes es prioridad de Julio Hernández." *Listín USA*, July 29–August 4. New York: CUNY Dominican Studies Institute Archives.

Allassan, Fadel. 2022. "Rep. Adriano Espaillat Pushing to Join Congressional Black Caucus." *Axios*, February 15. www.axios.com/2022/02/15/adriano-espaillat-black-caucus

Aparicio, Ana. 2006. *Dominican Americans and the Politics of Empowerment*. Gainesville: University Press of Florida.

Aponte, Sarah. 1999. *Dominican Migration to the United States, 1970–1997: An Annotated Bibliography*. New York: CUNY Dominican Studies Institute.

Aquino, Fernando. 2021. "Dominicans and the Political Realm of Latinidad in New York City." In *Latinidad at the Crossroads: Insights into Latinx Identity in the Twenty-First Century*, ed. Amanda Ellen Gerke and Luisa María González Rodríguez. Boston: Brill Rodopi, 66–83.

Arroyo, José. 1992. "Oficiales electos no irán a parada irlandesa sin gays." *Noticias del Mundo*, February 26. Anthony Stevens-Acevedo Archival Collection. New York: CUNY Dominican Studies Institute Archives.

Atanay, Reginaldo. 1992. "Dominicanos celebran la Restauración." *El Diario, La Prensa*, August 16. Rutgers University Libraries.

Batista, Frank. 1991. "Dominicans Come of Age." *The Village Voice*, September 3. New York: CUNY Dominican Studies Institute Archives.

Block, Alan A. 1989. "Violence, Corruption, and Clientelism: The Assassination of Jesús de Galíndez, 1956." *Social Justice* 16(2): 64–88. https://www-jstor-org.bcc.ezproxy.cuny.edu/stable/29766464?seq=3

Bredderman, Will. 2017. "Dominican-Born Congressman Defends His Home's Country Immigration Policies While Attacking Trump." May 10. https://observer.com/2017/05/adriano-espaillat-dominican-republic-haitians-immigration-deportation-undocumented-donald-trump/

Brown, Susan K., and Frank D. Bean. 2016. "Migration Status and Political Knowledge among Latino Immigrants." *The Russell Sage Foundation Journal of Social Sciences* 2(3): 22–41. www.jstor.org/stable/10.7758/rsf.2016.2.3.02

Bueno Vásquez, Michelle, Yalidy Matos, and Domingo Morel. 2022. "Afro-Latino Politicians Could Bridge the African America-Latino Divide." *The Washington Post*, October 25. www.washingtonpost.com/politics/2022/10/25/latino-racism-dominicans-congress/

Butten, Isabel. 1996a. "Activista dominicano busca ser asambleísta." *El Diario/La Prensa*, June 14. New York: CUNY Dominican Studies Institute Archives.

———. 1996b. "Expectativas de hispanos por las primarias." *El Diario/La Prensa*, September 11. New York: CUNY Dominican Studies Institute Archives.

Campbell, Colin. 2012. "Mark Levine Racking Up Club Endorsement in Shadow State Senate Race." *Observer*, May 24. https://observer.com/2012/05/mark-levine-racking-up-club-endorsements-in-shadow-state-senate-race/

Campo, Iban. 1995. "Política desde NY." *Listín Diario*, June. New York: CUNY Dominican Studies Institute Archives.

———. 1996a. "Campaña política en Nueva York: A 80 grados Farhenheit." *Listín Diario*, April 28. New York: CUNY Dominican Studies Institute Archives.

———. 1996b. "Consejal Guillermo Linares defiende intereses dominicanos en Ayuntamiento de Nueva York." *Listín Diario*, May 21. New York: CUNY Dominican Studies Institute Archives.

Casimir, Leslie. 2000. "Foreign-Born Pols Aim to Make Voices Heard." *News and Views*, August 24. New York: CUNY Dominican Studies Institute Archives.

Chacón, Héctor V. 1990. "El desfile dominicano. Líderes se acusan: Elecciones dudosas." *Listín USA*. New York: CUNY Dominican Studies Institute Archives.

Citizens Union. 2009. "2009 City Council District 10 Primary." https://citizensunion.org/portfolio-item/2009-city-council-district-10-primary/

CLACLS. 2021. "Latino Voters Registration Rates Reached an All-Time High in the 2020 Presidential Election." https://clacls.gc.cuny.edu/2021/05/10/latino-voter-registration-rates-reached-an-all-time-high-in-the-2020-presidential-election/

Coltin, Jeff. 2022. "How Rep. Adriano Espaillat Built the Squadriano." *City & State New York*, September 12. www.cityandstateny.com/politics/2022/09/how-rep-adriano-espaillat-built-squadriano/376969/

Cruz, David. 2021. "Dominican New Yorkers Broaden Political Base as More Gain the Right to Vote." *Gothamist*, May 4. https://gothamist.com/news/dominican-new-yorkers-broaden-political-base-more-gain-right-vote

Cruz Tejada, Miguel. 2018. "Adriano Espaillat retira apoyo a Marisol Alcantara." *Al Momento*, September 9. https://almomento.net/nueva-york-espaillat-rechaza-ataques-de-senadora-le-retira-su-apoyo/

Dana, Marie-Claude. 1992. "De Franco a Trujillo: L'éthique de la résistance." *Le Monde Diplomatique*, March. www.monde-diplomatique.fr/1992/03/DANA/44264

Dao, James. 1992. "Angered by Police Killing, a Neighborhood Erupts." *The New York Times*, July 7. www.nytimes.com/1992/07/07/nyregion/angered-by-police-killing-a-neighborhood-erupts.html

De La Hoz, Felipe. 2021. "The Growth of Dominican Political Power in New York." *Gotham Gazette*. www.gothamgazette.com/state/10283-growth-dominican-political-power-new-york-city-espaillat-reynoso

Domínguez, Adalberto. 1999. "Critica políticos RD sólo van NY a buscar." *El Nacional*, January 30. New York: CUNY Dominican Studies Institute Archives.

———. 2001. "Confía Bush reforme ley inmigración." *El Nacional*, January 4. New York: CUNY Dominican Studies Institute Archives.

Dominican American National Roundtable (DANR). 2004. "A Study of Dominican-American Voter Capacity." *City College*. New York: CUNY Dominican Studies Institute Archives.

Dominican Today. 2023. "US Lifts Travel Alert for the Dominican Republic over Racism Accusations, But Crime Warning Remains Active." April 25. https://dominicantoday.com/dr/tourism/2023/04/25/us-lifts-travel-alert-for-the-dominican-republic-over-racism-accusations-but-crime-warning-remains-active/

Dominicanos USA. 2017. "Opportunities to Engage the Dominican American Community." PDF.

Escotto, Rafael. 1990. "El peligro de ser taxista." *Listín USA*, December 3. New York: CUNY Dominican Studies Institute Archives.

Espaillat, Adriano. 2017. "Congressmember Adriano Espaillat Press Release." https://espaillat.house.gov/media/press-releases/congressman-adriano-espaillat-commends-guillermo-linares-appointment-lead-new

Ferrero, María Dolores, and Matilde Eiroa. 2016. "La oposición antitrujillista, la Legión del Caribe y José Figueres de Costa Rica (1944–1949)." *Revista Complutense de Historia de América* 42: 175–201.

Garcia-Rios, Sergio I., and Matt A. Barreto. 2016. "Politicized Immigrant Identity, Spanish-Language Media and Political Mobilization in 2012." *The Russell Sage Foundation Journal of the Social Sciences* 2(3): 78–96. www.jstor.org/stable/10.7758/rsf.2016.2.3.05

Govtrack. "Rep. Adriano Espaillat's 2019 Report Card." www.govtrack.us/congress/members/adriano_espaillat/412718/report-card/2019

Graham, Pamela. 1996. "Reimagining the Nation and Defining the District: Dominican Migration and Transnational Politics." *Center for Migration Studies* 13(4): 91–125. https://doi.org/10.1111/j.2050-411X.1996.tb00156.x

Guillén, Disraeli. 1990a. "Cree que los dominicanos necesitan de un concejal." *Listín USA*, December 3. New York: CUNY Dominican Studies Institute Archives.

———. 1990b. "Pide más apoyo a funcionarios de la administración Dinkins." *Listín USA*, December 3. New York: CUNY Dominican Studies Institute Archives

———. 1990–1991. "Renta y delincuencia perjudican los negocios." *Listín USA*, December 27–January 3. New York: CUNY Dominican Studies Institute Archives.

———. 1992. "Venganza en el Alto Manhattan: dominicanos cobrarán cuentas al Concejal Linares." *Anthony Stevens-Acevedo Archival Collection.* New York: CUNY Dominican Studies Institute Archives.

Hammer, Bettina, and Craig Kafura. 2019. "Republicans and Democrats in Different Worlds on Immigration." *Chicago Council on Global Affairs.* www.jstor.org/stable/resrep21289

Harlem World. 2022. "Uptown's Ydanis Rodriguez Talks TLC's Role in the Taxi Medallion Crisis." www.harlemworldmagazine.com/uptowns-ydanis-rodriguez-talks-tlcs-role-in-the-taxi-medallion-crisis/

Hernández, José María. 1995a. "Vaticinan habría retorno masivo hacia RD." *El Nacional*, April 23. New York: CUNY Dominican Studies Institute Archives.

———. 1995b. "Enfrentarían planes discriminatorios." *El Nacional*, April 23. New York: CUNY Dominican Studies Institute Archives.

Hernández, Ramona, and Francisco L. Rivera-Batiz. 2003. *Dominicans in the United States: A Socioeconomic Profile 2000.* New York: CUNY Dominican Studies Institute. www.columbia.edu/~flr9/documents/Dominicans_in_the _united_states_2003.pdf

Hernández, Ramona, Francisco L. Rivera-Batiz, and Sidie S. Sisay. 2022a. *Dominicans in the United States: A Socioeconomic Profile 2022.* New York: CUNY Dominican Studies Institute. www.columbia.edu/~flr9/ documents/Dominicans%20in%20the%20US%20Socioeconomic-Profile-2022%20final.pdf

Hernández, Ramona, Pedro Ortega, Nancy Sohler, and Sarah Marrara. 2022b. *Understanding COVID-19 among People of Dominican Descent in the U.S.: A Comparison of New York, New Jersey, Florida, Massachusetts, Pennsylvania, Rhode Island, and Connecticut.* New York: CUNY Dominican Studies Institute. www.ccny.cuny.edu/sites/default/files/2022-01/Understanding-Covid-19.pdf

Hicks, Jonathan P. 1998a. "Democratic Camps Expected to Clash again in an Assembly Race." *The New York Times*, April 6. New York: CUNY Dominican Studies Institute Archives.

———. 1998b. "Personal Rivalry Shadows Assembly Race." New York: CUNY Dominican Studies Institute Archives.

———. 2003. "In Washington Heights, a Race Has a Familiar Look." *The New York Times*, August 28. New York: CUNY Dominican Studies Institute Archives.

Holocaust Sources in Contest. "Dominican Republic Settlement Association, Sosúa: Heaven in the Caribbean." https://perspectives.ushmm.org/item/dominican-republic-settlement-association-sosua-haven-in-the-caribbean

Huddy, Leonie, Lilliana Mason, and S. Nechama Horwitz. 2016. "Political Identity Convergence: On Being Latino, Becoming a Democrat, and Getting Active." *The Russell Sage Foundation Journal of the Social Sciences* 2(3): 205–228. www.jstor.org/stable/10.7758/rsf.2016.2.3.11

Jiménez Polanco, Jacqueline. 1999a. "La representación política de las mujeres en América Latina." *América Latina Hoy* 22: 69–92. https://gredos.usal.es/handle/10366/72445?show=full

———. 1999b. *Los partidos políticos en la República Dominicana: Actividad electoral y desarrollo organizativo*. Santo Domingo: Editora Centenario.

———. 2011. "Women's Quotas in the Dominican Republic: Advances and Detractions." In Diffusion of Gender Quotas in Latin America and Beyond: Advances and Setbacks in the Last Two Decades, ed. Adriana Piatty-Crocker. New York: Peter Lang Publishing, 130–150. https://drive.google.com/file/d/1T1WSHkamLSCYkZmTgP9WpVPdUKRcWSDO/view?ths=true

Jiménez Polanco, Jacqueline, and Ernesto Sagás. 2023. *Dominican Politics in the Twenty First Century: Continuity and Change*. New York: Routledge.

Jones-Correa, Michael, and James A. McCann. 2013. "The Effects of Naturalization and Documentation Status on the Participation of Latino Immigrants." In *Annual Meeting of the American Political Science Association*, August 28–September 1.

Jordan, Howard. 1997. "Dominicans in New York: Getting a Slice of the Apple." *NACLA Report on the Americas*. March–April. 30(5): 37–42. New York: CUNY Dominican Studies Institute Archives.

———. 2001. "Dominicans Face Off in Manhattan." *Newsday.com*, June 7, New York: CUNY Dominican Studies Institute Archives.

Kochman, Ben. 2014. "Tarnished Bronx Politician, Albany Informer, Nelson Castro Escaped Prison for Perjury, Vows New Career Selling Lightbulbs." *New York Daily News*, November 17. www.nydailynews.com/new-york/bronx/tarnished-bronx-lawmaker-dodges-prison-time-perjury-article-1.2014121

Krohn-Hansen, Christian. 2013. *Making New York Dominican*. Philadelphia: University of Pennsylvania Press.

Larancuent, Wilfredo N., Álvarez-López, Luis, and Miriam Mejía. 1991. "Actitud de los Votantes en Washington Heights." New York: Centro de Estudios Dominicanos. CUNY Dominican Studies Institute Archives.

Latino Decision. 2015. "Opportunities to Engage the Dominican American Community: Dominicanos USA." PDF.

Leighley, Jan, and Jonathan Nagler. 2016. "Latino Electoral Participation: Variations on Demographics and Ethnicity." *The Russell Sage Foundation Journal of the Social Sciences* 2(3): 148–164. www.jstor. org/stable/10.7758/rsf.2016.2.3.08

Lescaille, Fernando. 1992. *Dominican Political Empowerment.* New York: Dominican Public Policy Project. New York: CUNY Dominican Studies Institute Archives.

Lewis-Beck, Michael S., and Mary Stegmair. 2016. "The Hispanic Immigrant Voter and the Classic American Voter: Presidential Support in the 2012 Election." *The Russel Sage Foundation Journal of the Social Sciences* 2(3): 165–181. www.jstor.org/stable/10.7758/rsf.2016.2.3.09

Listín USA. 1990–1991. "Cientos de dominicanos asesinados por causa de las drogas en NY." December 27–January 3. New York: CUNY Dominican Studies Institute Archives.

Maisel, Todd. 2020. "These People Deserve to be Heard: NYC Council Makes Efforts to Allow Immigrants to Vote." *AMNY*, January 23. www. amny.com/politics/these-people-deserve-to-be-heard-nyc-council-makes-effort-to-allow-immigrants-to-vote/

Manuel de Dios Unanue. 1999. *El caso Galíndez: Los vascos en los servicios de inteligencia de los Estados Unidos.* Txalaparta, S.L.

Matos, Yalidy, and Domingo Morel. 2021. "Dominican Political Incorporation in the United States." *Latino Studies* 20: 67–93.

Mota Zurdo, David. 2020. "El caso Galíndez en la prensa estadounidense." In *El historiador y la prensa: Homenaje a José Miguel Delgado Idarreta*, eds. Nadia Aït-Bachir, Raquel Irizarri Gutiérrez, Víctor Rodrítuez Infiesta, Rebeca Rivera Ruiz, and José Miguel Delgado Idarreta. Burgos: Universidad Isabel I. https://dialnet.unirioja.es/servlet/artic ulo?codigo=7654429

Moya Pons, Frank. 1995. *The Dominican Republic: A National History.* New York: Hispaniola Books.

Neuman, William. 2016. "Adriano Espaillat Is in Position to Replace Rangel and Become First Dominican in Congress." *The New York Times*, June 29. www.nytimes.com/2016/06/29/nyregion/adriano-espaillat-charles-rangel-first-dominican-in-congress.html

Newman, Maria. 1992. "New Leadership Forms in a Crucible of Violence." *The New York Times*, July 11. www.nytimes.com/1992/07/11/nyregion/new-leadership-forms-in-a-crucible-of-violence.html

Niedzwiadek, Nick. 2016. "Alcantara Wins Race to Replace Espaillat, Bolster IDC." *Politico*, September 14. www.politico.com/states/new-york/alb any/story/2016/09/alcantara-wins-race-to-replace-fellow-latino-espaillat-105438

Noe-Bustamante, Luis, Abby Budiman, and Hugo Lopez. 2020. "Where Latinos Have the Most Eligible Voters in the 2020 Election." *Pew Research Center*. www.pewresearch.org/fact-tank/2020/01/31/where-latinos-have-the-most-eligible-voters-in-the-2020-election/

Novas, José. C. 2018. "Éxodo, luchas y exilio: Crónica sobre la colonia dominicana en Nueva York, 1919–1965." August. New York: Dominican Studies Institute Library.

Odato, James M. 2014. "New York Lawmaker Gabriela Rosa Pleads Guilty to Felonies." *Times Union*, June 27. www.timesunion.com/local/article/New-York-lawmaker-Gabriela-Rosa-pleads-guilty-to-5585839.php

Ortiz, Keidy. 2023a. "Sabina Matos Vies for Victory in Rhode Island Special Election." *Axios*, March 13. www.axios.com/2023/03/13/sabina-matos-dominican-congress-rhode-island

———. 2023b. "Just One Dominican American Serves in Congress, But That Could Soon Change." *Axios*, September 5. www.axios.com/2023/09/05/domican-american-congress-sabina-matos-adrian-espaillat

Palante. 1973. "Pueblo dominicano en N.Y protesta represión Balaguer." February 15-28,5:3,1-3, 10-11. CUNY Dominican Studies Institute Library.

Paulino, Edward. 2016. *Dividing Hispaniola: The Dominican Republic's Border Campaign against Haiti, 1930–1961*. Pittsburgh: University of Pittsburgh Press.

Paybarah, Azi. 2012. "At a Rally to Boost Black and Latino Representation in Congress, Espaillat Cautions against Redistricting 'Crackers'." *Politico*, March 12. www.politico.com/states/new-york/albany/story/2012/03/at-a-rally-to-boost-black-and-latino-representation-in-congress-espaillat-cauti ons-against-redistricting-crackers-000000

Paybarah, Azi, and Conor Skelding. 2016. "Espaillat Claims 'Historic' Victory in Race to Replace Rangel." *Politico*, June 29. www.politico.com/states/new-york/albany/story/2016/06/espaillat-declares-victory-in-race-to-replace-rangel-103359

Pereira, Ivan. 2014. "Human Rights Project Releases Report Card on City Council." *AMNY*, March 25. www.amny.com/news/human-rights-project-releases-report-card-on-city-council-1-7502339/

Pessar, Patricia R. 1995. *A Visa for a Dream: Dominicans in the United States*. Boston: MA: Allyn and Bacon.

Pew Research Center. 2023. "Facts on Hispanics of Dominican Origin in the United States, 2021." August 16. www.pewresearch.org/hispanic/fact-sheet/us-hispanics-facts-on-dominican-origin-latinos/

Pipper, J. Weston. 2015. "What Do Dominican Americans Really Want? *The Atlantic*, August 28.

Potochnick, Stephanie, and Mary Stegmaier. 2020. "Latino Political Participation by Citizenship Status and Immigrant Generation." *Social Science Quarterly* 101(2): 527–544.

Ricourt, Milagros. 2002. *Dominicans in New York City: Power from the Margins*. New York: Routledge. https://archive.org/details/dominicansinn ewy0000rico .

Ring, Harry. 1966. "O. E. Moscoso, Dominican Patriot, Dies in New York." *The Militant* 30(47): 5. www.marxists.org/history/dominican-republic/ 1966/obituary.htm

Rivera, Ray, and Barbaro Michael. 2009. "City Councilman Steps Down as Criminal Charges Loom." *The New York Times*, July 14. www.nytimes. com/2009/07/15/nyregion/15resign.html

Sachs, Susan. 2001. "Give Me Your Tired, Your Poor, Your Vote." *The New York Times*, April 8. New York: CUNY Dominican Studies Institute Archives.

Sagás, Ernesto, and Sintia E. Molina, eds. 2004. *Dominican Migration: Transnational Perspectives*. Gainesville: University Press of Florida.

Sánchez, Chelsey. 2018. "Rematch of Tight Manhattan Senate Primary Takes Shape in Different Political Environment." *CITY*, August 10. https://mail. google.com/mail/u/0/#search/jessy/FMfcgzGrbRZxtfxNDsLGjtLztMLLG rJF?projector=1&messagePartId=0.4

Santana, Nelson, and Sarah Aponte. 2019. *The CUNY Dominican Studies Institute Library: Bringing the Community to the Academic Library*. New York: City University of New York. https://academicworks.cuny.edu/ cgi/viewcontent.cgi?article=1112&context=bx_pubs

Sears, David O., Felix Danbold, and Vanessa M. Zavala. 2016. "Incorporation of Latino Immigrants into the American Party System." *The Russell Sage Foundation Journal of the Social Sciences* 2(3): 183–204. www.jstor.org/ stable/10.7758/rsf.2016.2.3.10?seq=1&cid=pdf-reference#references_tab_ contents

Sierra, José Alduey. 1991. "Dinkins anuncia recortes y más impuestos." *Listín USA*, February 7–13. New York: CUNY Dominican Studies Institute Archives.

Smith, Robert Courtney. 2017. "'Don't Let the Illegals Vote!': The Myths of Illegal Latino Voters and Voter Fraud in Contested Local Immigrant Integration." *The Russell Sage Foundation Journal of the Social Sciences* 3(4): 148–175. www.jstor.org/stable/10.7758/rsf.2017.3.4.09?searchT ext=&searchUri=&ab_segments=&searchKey=&refreqid=fastly-defa ult%3A7d4628841ad50f628f8be86d3c16ddfd

Sosar, David P. 2018. "Hispanic Voters, State and Local Elections: How to Awake the Sleeping Giant." *Review of History and Political Science* 6(1): 1–11.

Stevens-Acevedo, Anthony. 1991. "Linares Poised for Victory in Council Race, Leads in Money, Endorsements and Volunteers." New York: CUNY Dominican Studies Institute Archives.

———. 1992a. "Ideas Para el Programa de Campaña." *Amigos de Guillermo Linares*. New York: CUNY Dominican Studies Institute Archives.

———. 1992b. "Los dominicanos de Nueva York y el Censo del 1990." New York: CUNY Dominican Studies Institute Archives.

———. 1992c. "América, no culpes más a Washington Heights." New York: CUNY Dominican Studies Institute Archives.

———. 1992d. "Gran marcha por una mejor educación y por el futuro de la juventud." New York: CUNY Dominican Studies Institute Archives.

———. 1992e. "Stevens propone el nombre de Gregorio Luperón para una nueva escuela en el Alto Manhattan." New York: CUNY Dominican Studies Institute Archives.

———. 1992f. "Renewal of Affirmative Action Initiatives in CS D6." New York: CUNY Dominican Studies Institute Archives.

———. 1993a. "Una junta escolar más conservadora." New York: CUNY Dominican Studies Institute Archives.

———. 1993b. "Sectores de comunidad dominicana reaccionan ante intervencionismo de asambleísta Murtaugh." New York: CUNY Dominican Studies Institute Archives.

———. 1993c. "Piden más empleos para dominicanos en el distrito escolar 6." New York: CUNY Dominican Studies Institute Archives.

———. 1993d. "Otro rotativo declara a Linares mejor concejal del año." New York: CUNY Dominican Studies Institute Archives.

———. 1995. "Liderazgo comunal y generaciones en la población dominicana de Nueva York (Reflexión pesimista para un futuro mejor)." New York: CUNY Dominican Studies Institute Archives.

Stevens-Acevedo, Anthony, Tom Weterings, and Leonor Álvarez Francés. 2013. *Juan Rodriguez and the Beginnings of New York City*. New York: CUNY Dominican Studies Institute.

The Bronx Free Press. 2014. "On a Registration Roll. Enlistando registros." May 29. https://thebronxfreepress.com/on-a-registration-roll-enlistando-registros/

The Militant. 1962. "Appeal Made for Anti-Trujillo Exiles." 26(17): 4. www.marxists.org/history/dominican-republic/1962/exiles.htm

———. 1966. "New York March Backs Dominican Revolution." 30(18): 2. www.marxists.org/history/dominican-republic/1966/new-york-march.htm

The Washington Heights Citizen & The Inwood News. 1991. "Dominican Array for New Council Seat". December–January. New York: CUNY Dominican Studies Institute Archives.

Torres-Saillant, Silvio, and Ramona Hernández. 1998. *The Dominican Americans*. Connecticut: Greenwood Press. https://archive.org/details/dominicanamerica0000torr

Union Square Awards. 2002. "Dominicans 2000: Pre-University Program." http://unionsq.dreamhosters.com/social-justice-orgs/34-2002/258-dominic ans-2000--pre-university-program.html

U.S. Census Bureau. 2016. *American Community Survey.* https://data.census. gov/table?q=dominicans+2016&tid=ACSSPP1Y2016.S0201

Vega, Bernardo. 1984. *La migración española de 1939 y los inicios del marxismo leninismo en la República Dominicana.* Santo Domingo: Fundación Cultural Dominicana.

Viñuales, David. 1997. "La historia de pasión y división en la política." *Listín Diario,* August 10. New York: CUNY Dominican Studies Institute Archives.

———. 1998. "La historia se repite en Washington Heights, pero ahora es al revés." *Listín Diario,* April 11. New York: CUNY Dominican Studies Institute Archives.

Wallenfeldt, Jeff. 2022. "Los Angeles Riots of 1992." *Britannica.* www.bri tannica.com/event/Los-Angeles-Riots-of-1992

WNBC/Channel 4. 1992. "Washington Heights Protest." July 3. www.yout ube.com/watch?v=d6SCk3F1OAU   www.youtube.com/watch?v=wH_2 Roelsw4

Yingling, Charlton W. 2013. "To the Reconciliation of All Dominicans: The Transnational Trials of Dominican Exiles in the Trujillo Era." In *Crossing Boundaries: Ethnicity, Race, and National Belonging in a Transnational World,* ed. Brian D. Behnken and Simon Wendt. Maryland: Lexington Books, 39–53. https://mail.google.com/mail/u/0/#search/jhensen/KtbxLrj NZhhNvstNvcJcGcPfPqvNJXnJPL?projector=1&messagePartId=0.2

Index

Printed in the United States
by Baker & Taylor Publisher Services